Checkertails

The 325th Fighter Group in the Second World War

By
Ernest R. McDowell
Color By
Don Greer and Tom Tullis

squadron/signal publications

The 325th Fighter Group flew three fighter types during its existance: the Curtiss P-40 Warhawk, Republic P-47 Thunderbolt and North American P-51 Mustang.

Dedication

This book is dedicated to Kenn C. Rust, who got me started. To all the men who served in the USAAC, USAAF, and USAF and especially to all members of the 325th Fighter Group."Bless 'em all."

ISBN 0-89747--316-7

If you have any photographs of aircraft, armor, soldiers or ships of any nation, particularly wartime snapshots, why not share them with us and help make Squadron/Signal's books all the more interesting and complete in the future. Any photograph sent to us will be copied and the original returned. The donor will be fully credited for any photos used. Please send them to:

Squadron/Signal Publications, Inc.
1115 Crowley Drive.
Carrollton, TX 75011-501010

Acknowledgments

Members Of The 325th Fighter Group:

Gordon C. Austin	Robert M. Barkey
Robert L. Baseler	Ernest H.Beverly
Ray Brooks	J. W. Cannon
William K. Carswell	Lewis W."Bill" Chick,Jr.
H. L. Cramer	Barrie S. Davis
Cecil 0. Dean	Ed Doss
Paul B.Dowd	Benjamin H. Emmert, Jr.
Jack Evans	Arthur C. Fiedler, Jr.
Ralph L.Fort	Ira Grandel
Herschel H. Green	Roy Hogg
Paul Hudson	Wayne L. Lowry
Donald MacDonald	Paul Maret
George Ording	F. Patt
Dan Penrod	Stan Rosen
Mark Rowley	L. Schneider
J. Strauss	William Stolarczyk
C. E. Swann	Ralph G. "Zack" Taylor, Jr.
Felix "Pic" Vidal	John C.A. Watkins
Stanley Wilson	

Aviation Historians:

Joe Consliglio	James V. Crow
Larry Davis	Jeff Ethell
Gary L. Fry	Royal Frey
C.L. Glines	William N. Hess
Richard M. Hill	Robert C. Jones
Art Krieger	George J. Letzter
Kenn C. Rust	David C. Weatherill
Phil Yant	Dwayne Tabatt

Without their help this book would not have been possible.

Introduction

325th Fighter Group

Formed as the 325th Fighter Group on 24 June 1942, the new group was activated on 20 July under general order number 50 issued by 1st Air Force headquarters, Eastern Defense Command with activation taking place on 3 August 1942.

Officers and enlisted men were detached from the 79th Fighter Group under the command of Major Leonard C. Lydon to form the nucleus of the new fighter group. The group headquarters and 317th Squadron were based at Theodore Green Field, Hillsgrove, Rhode Island, the 318th was sent to Grenier Field, Manchester, New Hampshire and the 319th deployed to Renschler Field, Hartford, Connecticut. Additional personnel was drawn from various service schools, Officer Candidate Schools, replacement pools and inductees who had completed basic training. Some of the new officers from OCS were given intensified courses in chemical warfare, camouflage, intelligence, and other specialist areas. Enlisted men attended lectures, viewed training films, drilled and received on the job training in their new assignments. Pilots practiced formation flying, aerobatics, navigation, instrument flying and aerial gunnery.

The activities of the 319th Squadron during this period may be cited as more or less typical. Initially, the squadron consisted of 178 enlisted men under the command of Captain Lawrence E. Oldham, who was the only officer attached to the 319th at the time. Major Robert I. Baseler arrived on 26 August to assume command as pilots began to trickle in to the 319th.

Bob Baseler was a tall, gangling, soft spoken redhead, an easy going individual with a keen sense of humor. He had earned his wings at Kelly Field, Texas on 1 February 1939. His first duty was as a pursuit pilot with the 94th Pursuit Squadron, the famed Hat-In-The-Ring squadron of WW I fame, which was flying P-35s and P-36s at that time. One of the best pilots in the squadron was Neel E. Kearby and Bob got to know and admire him. He asked Neel to help him perfect his dogfight fighting techniques and Neel agreed, but to make it interesting suggested that a wager be made on the outcome of each session. Bob paid off on a fairly regular basis the first month and then began to hold his own but he never did win back all of the money he lost. He always considered it as money well spent. Later in the war Neel Kearby, who became commanding officer of the 348th Fighter Group in the Pacific theater, was awarded the Medal Of Honor and had accounted for twenty-two enemy aircraft destroyed before losing his life in combat.

A flight of 319th Fighter Squadron pilots pose in full flight gear at Hillsgrove, Rhode Island in December of 1942, just before the 325th departed for North Africa Only two men in this group survived the war (John C.A. Watkins)

Armorers load the. 50 caliber wing guns of a P-40F Warhawk of the 325th Fighter Group on the deck of USS RANGER while enroute to North Africa. (Checkertail Clan)

After leaving the 94th PS, Baseler was sent to the 16th Pursuit Group at Albrook in the Panama Canal Zone where he gained additional experience flying Curtiss P-36 and P-40 fighters. He was then sent to the 325th Fighter Group to command the 319th Fighter Squadron.

As soon as Major Baseler took command he intensified flight training and began to pass on his knowledge of tactics to his new charges. As part of their training they flew regular patrols over the New England coastal areas under command of the Boston Air Defense Wing. On 5 October 1942, they were transferred to Hillsgrove at which time squadron strength stood at 29 officers and 312 enlisted men.

Lieutenant George B. Gingras was appointed commanding officer of the 318th on 3 August 1942, but the 317th did not get a commander until 1 September, when James E. Tucker assumed command, but he was replaced by Captain Jack C. West on 7 October. When Bob Baseler moved up to the headquarters staff on 14 November, Captain Walter V. Radovich replaced him as commander of 319th squadron. Major Lydon, having seen the 325th through the initial stages was replaced by Lieutenant Colonel Gordon H. Austin on 10 December, who immediately took steps to bring the group up to a combat readiness state in anticipation of the order to move it to a combat theater, which was not long in coming. Special order Number 1 dated 1 January 1943, by Headquarters Boston Air Defense Command, called for the group to proceed via rail without delay to Langley Field, Virginia. The move was to be a permanent change of station. Personnel were allowed 175 pounds of luggage, limited to a foot locker and a barracks or B-4 bag. All personnel were put on alert with the pilots ordered to move out on 2 January 1943.

Due to a snafu, the 318th's orders stated that the pilots uniform of the

Pilots of the 319th Fighter Squadron pose for a group portrait while aboard RANGER. The P-40s had engine exhaust covers in place and had a protective coating on the canopy glass. (Paul Maret)

The 317th Fighter Squaron also lined up for a group shot while aboard USS RANGER. The squadron commander, Herschel H. Green is at the far right standing. (C. O. Dean)

Lieutenant Colonel Gordon H. Austin, group commander (right), Captain Durgin USS RANGER commander (center) and Major Tinker, group operations officer (left) discuss the upcoming launch from USS RANGER just before the ship arrived off North Africa. (G.C. Austin)

day would be complete combat flight gear despite the fact that the transfer was to be a rail move. The 318th assembled fully clad for flight to board the busses and were taken to the South Boston railroad depot. Needless to say the civilians in the station were surprised to see a fighter squadron marching into the station waiting room carrying parachutes, gas masks, pistols, B-4 bags, canteens and other gear. Lieutenant Bryant noted they were the center of attention, took out his ocarina and rendered a rousing "Over There." The rest of the squadron gathered around him and put on an impromptu concert of WW I favorites which the crowd of over a hundred fellow travelers seemed to enjoy. A few men slipped out to buy liquid refreshments for the long dry trip. The order to board the train ended the show and the crowd gave them a big hand and shouted words of encouragement. A few of the bold decided to kiss the girls good-bye whether they knew them or not.

Upon boarding the train the 318th found themselves in luck as they were the first to board the troop train. They quickly settled in the plush parlor car with its thick leather swivel seats, much to the chagrin of the 317th and 318th pilots who arrived later and had to be content with coach and baggage car accommodations. Traveling all night they arrived in Norfolk, Virginia at 1100 the next morning. There they were quickly checked into quarters and put through a short but intensive train-

ing session.

New P-40Fs awaited them and they were told that they would be ferried by aircraft carrier to a point off the coast of North Africa where they'd fly their planes off the carrier to their new base. Since none of the pilots had ever flown off a carrier deck they were put through a special training program designed to allow them to make simulated takeoffs, as though they were taking off from the USS RANGER's flight deck. Working with naval officers, a runway at Langley was marked off with a series of lines which indicated the maximum permissible takeoff run for a P-40 from the flight deck of the RANGER. These lines took into account the carrier's speed of 25 knots, varying wind velocities over the deck, loss of drag on the aircraft as it left the deck and drop off speed increase for a deck with the bow approximately fifty feet above the waterline. Each pilot had to be airborne by the time he reached the line prescribed for the wind and other conditions at time of takeoff and each was required to make at least two simulated takeoffs successfully. Takeoffs were made with internal fuel only, empty belly tanks, full power, and flaps set at 15 degrees. Some pilots managed to get in an extra practice takeoff. Major Baseler recalled that he got off cleanly on both tries and encountered no difficulties. Training was completed on 6 January 1943, and next morning the pilots flew to Naval Air Station Norfolk , taxied their P-40s to the dock alongside the RANGER so they could be hoisted aboard the carrier. The flight echelon of the group boarded the RANGER and were shown to their quarters by the ship's crew. The RANGER cast off on 8 January 1943, at 1130 and put to sea with a convoy of six destroyers, a cruiser and a tanker. The next day the seas were heavy and most of the 325th pilots suffered sea sickness in varying degrees but the weather was good the following day and it warmed up enough to call for a change to summer uniforms. They were briefed on flying conditions in North Africa. Navy chow was excellent and they had a chance to tour the huge ship and swap yarns with the RANGER's crew.

More than a few pilots were seen pacing off the distance from their takeoff point to the bow. Major Baseler felt that he could stand at the starting point and spit across the bow despite the wind blowing over the deck. Yet, the Navy had allotted the Army pilots 425 feet of deck space even though they only allowed their own pilots 390 feet

After an uneventful crossing, the morning of 19 January found them within flight range of their destination, so the order the 325th was to hear for the first and only time was given, "Pilots, man your planes!" They took off and pointed their noses towards Cazes Aerodrome near Casablanca. All of the Warhawks got off cleanly. Major Baseler who led the second section of thirty-six noted that only two planes in the first section, led by Lieutenant Colonel Austin, dropped below deck level after getting off. Baseler cleared the deck with about fifty feet to spare and after a turn to clear his prop wash from the path of the pilot behind him, glanced back. The carrier looked about the size of his thumb nail. He prayed that the ship's navigator had given him the correct bearings because, while he felt fairly certain that he could find Africa ,he doubted that he could find the carrier again.

Gordon H. Austin -- Group Commander

Gordon H. Austin was commander of the 325th Fighter Group from 10 December 1942 until 5 July 1943. He was a popular leader who lead by doing everything he asked his men to do. Austin was born in Davenport, Iowa on 1 September 1913, and entered West Point in 1932, the year his father, Major General Gordon F.T. Austin retired from the Army. Gordon graduated from the academy in June of 1936 and was commissioned a 2nd Lieutenant and was posted to Randolph Field to undergo primary and basic flight training. He went through advanced training at Kelly Field and on competion of training in February of 1938 he was assigned to Bolling Field, Washington, DC. In May of 1940 he

P-40F Warhawks of the 325th Fighter Group taxi into position for launch from USS RANGER off North Africa on 19 January 1943. All the aircraft carried an American flag painted on the fuselage as a recognition marking. (Checkertail Clan)

was sent to Hickham Field, Hawaii, where on 1 December 1940, he activated and assumed command of the 47th Fighter Squadron at Wheeler Field. Major Austin had moved his squadron to Haleiwa Beach for gunnery training and on 7 December he and several members of his staff were returning from an inspection of ground gunnery facilities in an unarmed utility aircraft. He managed to slip into Wheeler and head for Haleiwa to get some of their P-40s into action since the Japanese had overlooked the base. The 47th Squadron was credited with eight enemy aircraft destroyed and four probables during the attack.

He then returned to the Zone of the Interior (ZI) to assume command of the 325th on 10 December 1942. As commander Gordy flew 100 combat hours in P-40s and was credited with three air-to-air victories during his tour.

Though Austin was happy in his role as commander of the 325th, he was ordered to take over the 319th Bombardment Group, which he vehemently contested. Finally, he was given a direct order to do so. The 319th was a Martin B-26 outfit that had been having a run of bad luck, losing a number of commanders in combat. He flew 115 combat hours in the Marauder and succeeded in getting the Group up to combat ready status.

Off To War -- Bill Lott

After completing combat training, the 325th received orders to depart for an overseas destination. Someone once said that intelligent men can read the same material but interpret it differently. And in this instance, history repeated itself.

When the 318th Squadron received the orders, we understood that we were to depart by train from Boston and on arrival at our destination, aircraft would be awaiting us which we would fly to an unknown destination without delay. Thus we departed Manchester dressed in full combat flying gear including flight suits, helmets, pistols, parachutes, etc. Needless to say, our arrival at South Station created quite a stir among the travelers. In a few minutes we were surrounded by a curious, intensely interested crowd who were uncertain what the pres-

ence of so many armed men signified. Upon learning that the squadron was bound for combat a party type mood blossomed spontaneously, accompanied by the ocarina playing of Lieutenant Bryant (one of the pilots who unfortunately was not fated to survive the war). Singing, dancing, taking nips from the profusion of proffered flasks and kissing pretty lasses was pretty much the order of the day and for a short time the war faded from our thoughts.

All good things must come to an end and perhaps because someone recalled that "a slip of the lip will sink a ship", we were ordered to board the train even though we were early. This was accomplished in short order and the best seats on the train were commandeered — interpretation: the luxurious parlor car was fully occupied by the 318th.

Shortly thereafter the 317th and 319th squadrons, having correctly interpreted the orders, arrived in Class A uniforms. Their arrival in conventional military garb drew little attention as they marched directly to the train and boarded. Chagrined that all the best seats were

A P-40F Warhawk of the 325th Fighter Group runs up its engine as it prepares to taxi into position on the wooden flight deck of USS RANGER. (Checkertail Clan)

Lieutenant Colonel Gordon Austin takes off from USS RANGER to lead the 325th to Casablanca. Some seventy P-40Fs of the 325th successfully launched from RANGER without incident. (Checkertail Clan)

already occupied, they were further annoyed that they had to travel in Class A uniforms while the 318th wore much more comfortable flight suits.

For the 318th it was a case of the "early bird gets the worm" and perhaps the thought that a little judicious misinterpretation of the written word can at times turn out to be a lot more fun. In the other two squadrons, the only muttering heard was, "How do I get out of this chicken outfit!"

Following an overnight trip from Boston, we arrived at Norfolk where we learned that we would go into combat with new P-40Fs instead of the older P-40Es we had flown at our New England bases. We also were informed that we would be loaded aboard a Navy aircraft carrier and launched from the carrier when we were within range of our overseas destination. As you can imagine, we were all agog at this news and training began immediately. This was accomplished by simply painting the outline of a carrier deck an the runway and ensuring that all pilots could takeoff within this distance. After all the pilots had successfully performed this maneuver, the Group was pronounced ready.

I recall very vividly that we taxied our aircraft right down the main street of Norfolk to the aircraft carrier RANGER, and I'm sure a lot of Norfolk people were bug-eyed to find our P-40s using their main drag. But that was only the first of many one time experiences that the group would encounter. As soon as we taxied up to the RANGER the aircraft, with the pilot still in the cockpit, was hoisted to the flight deck which was another experience that although completed safely, I could have done without.

During the voyage, I think each pilot stepped off the distance from our take-off point on the deck to the bow of the ship several times and each time it seemed to get shorter. Somehow our previous practice on the land runway did not prepare us for the big drop off at the end of the carrier deck to the sea below. While practicing on land, if one did not have flying speed by the time he reached the end of the carrier deck outlined an the runway, there was additional runway available. But on the carrier if you did not have flying speed by the time you reached the bow, there was nothing but a plunge to the ocean wa-a-ay below and a giant carrier right behind you coming on at 30 knots.

Bob Baseler, who as I recall was our Executive Officer unwittingly provided us with our war cry of "Shoot the Bastards." During the trip, Bob gave a rousing briefing emphasizing that our training was over and we would soon be facing the Germans. He wanted us to remember that we would have to "shoot the bastards" or they would

came back and shoot us. And although it elicited a lot of laughter at the time, we later remembered it and thus the 318th had its battle cry: "Shoot the bastards."

Finally came the announcement that tomorrow would be the big day. This was followed by the news that steak was on the menu for the evening mess which had some of us speculating about a last meal for the condemned. But Lady Luck smiled on the 325th and everyone got off ok albeit some looked pretty wobbly doing it.

As we joined up for the flight to Casablanca, and I looked back at the carrier, I realized exactly what every Navy pilot meant when he said that an aircraft carrier looked about the size of a postage stamp. I was extremely grateful that we would not have to return to it.

Major Cecil O. Dean

Dean, a native of Panama City, Florida, was a twenty year old Staff Sergeant pilot when he joined the 325th at Hillsgrove, Rhode Island. He was among the pilots selected to fly anti-submarine patrol out of Boston's Logan Airport which he recalled were uneventful. The night that the Coconut Grove night club caught fire he was at the club but had left before the tragic fire that took the life of cowboy movie star Buck Jones, along with more than fifty others.

Other events during this period were like the time one of the pilots forcibly removed a WAC mechanic from his plane when he caught her removing the glass cover of the fuel gauge with a hammer. Then there was the civilian gambler, a pro, who showed up in a military uniform and joined in their friendly poker game. When he was exposed as a tin horn he quickly lost his nice uniform, his money and was given a new version of the old Boston tea party. They heaved him into the bay — during January! One of his buddies, Flight Officer Bill Brookbank was assigned the top bunk on USS RANGER and a hot pipe carrying either steam or hot water passed just over the top of the bunk so that any time he rolled over he got scorched. As a result, he was given the name "Hotpipes" Taking off from RANGER was an experience never to be

Captain William M. Lott of the 318th Fighter Squadron is presented with the Distinguished Flying Cross (DFC) from General Atkinson later in the war. Bill Lott later said his most vivid memory of the war was taxiing down the streets of Norfolk, Virginia and being hoisted aboard USS RANGER for the trip to North Africa. (Checkertail Clan)

Colonel Austin poses with a group of pilots from the 325th. Austin is the third from right and directly behind him is Frank "Spot" Collins, the pilot credited with the group's first air-to-air kill. Collins would end the war an ace with a total of nine kills. (Checkertail Clan)

This P-40F named SWEET LAURIE II was flown by Flight Officer Bill H. Slattery of the 318th Fighter Squadron. Bill was one of the pilots who took part in the mission against the seaplane base on 1 June 1943. He was credited with three kills, a Bf 109, a Ju 52 and a Macchi 202. (Richard L. Davis via Dwayne Tabatt)

forgotten, but all went well and they were off to war. Dean had his ammo bays filled with Navy whiskey, towels, tax free jewelry, and steaks. Following the leaders after forming up, they headed for land and knew they were close when they spotted vapor trails. Most of the Group thought they were the RAF, instead it was the Germans who had arrived too early to ambush them and were leaving because of low fuel. Dean was one of four 325th Aces who scored victories with the Curtiss P-40 Warhawk, Republic P-47 Thunderbolt and North American P-51 Mustang. His total score was six.

North Africa

When the pilots landed at Cazes they were held there until 23 January when they were sent to Mediouna. The next day they flew a protective patrol for President Roosevelt's party and the following day, they flew on to Tafaraoui to join the others already there. The others had reached the base via various routes and methods of transportation, including any flights available via Florida, Trinidad, Puerto Rico, Brazil, Ascension Island and finally Africa. Portions of the trip were on commercial air lines and military flights. Others went via rail to the port of embarkation in New York harbor and boarded the USS LYON which took thirteen days to make the crossing.

On 29 January, Colonel Austin, Major Tinker and Lieutenant Watkins flew to Algiers to confer with Generals Doolittle and Spaatz. Early in February Colonel Austin led a flight of twenty aircraft to Youks Les Baines where they turned over the P-40s to the veteran 33rd Fighter Group, operating in Western Tunisia. These aircraft were replacements for the 33rd's war weary aircraft. Major Baseler led an additional twenty-four Warhawks and turned them over to Colonel Phillip Cochrane's Red Scarf guerrillas leaving the 325th with only twenty-eight aircraft of their own.

Lieutenant Colonel Austin in the cockpit of his P-40F named Lighthouse Louie. The two kill markings were kills scored on a mission flown on 28 June 1943. His ground crew, J.W. O'Neal and Waller are listed on the name plate under the windscreen.

Lieutenant William M. Lott's P-40F was named LOTTO-O which was a play on words of his last name. Bill shot down a Bf 109 while flying this P-40 on 20 May 1943. The aircraft also had an Arkansas Razorback hog painted on both sides of the nose. (via Dwayne Tabatt)

Colonel Austin met with Brigadier General James (Jimmy) Doolittle (center) and Colonel Fordyce, commander of the 320th Bomb Group, to discuss escort duties for the 325th at Montesquieu, Algeria. Two months later Colonel Austin would be transferred to take over command of a B-26 Marauder bomber group. (Gordon Austin)

On 11 February, the group suffered its first operational loss when Lieutenant George Gingras, the 318th Squadron's commander and his operations officer Lieutenant Joe Bloomer, had a mid-air collision while practicing a formation loop. Bloomer bailed out after Gingras's propeller cut off the tail of his P-40 but Gingras, for some unknown reason, failed to get out and he was killed when his Warhawk spun in from 6,000 feet.

At 0600 on 1 June 1943, thirty six P-40s, twelve from each squadron, took off on the best planned mission up to that time. Eight returned early, but the rest continued on to their target, the Italian seaplane base at Stangone, Sicily. The aircraft based there were being used to ferry supplies from the mainland to the Axis forces in North Africa. Therefore, it was a most vital target.

Attacking in waves, on the deck, flight after flight of Warhawks came in over the sea wall that protected the seaplane base from the open sea. The element of surprise was complete and the base was caught totally off guard.

Major Bob Baseler, who was credited with destruction of two sea-

(Left to Right) Captain Clem Crowley, Major Robert W. Myers and Major Everett B. Howe wait for group P-40s to return from a mission. Myers was the first P-40 pilot to take off with a 1,000 pound bomb and Howe was later shot down and spent the rest of the war as a POW. (John C.A. Watkins)

Gordy Austin volunteered to be a guinea pig and sample the first batch of moonshine from the prototype still built by John Watkins and Bunn Hearn at Montesquieu, Algeria. (John C.A. Watkins)

planes said afterwards, *"We just snuck up on them before anyone was up moving around and got out before they knew what hit them"*. Flight Officer Scott Leninger remarked *"We sounded reveille for that place today, but it was also taps for some of them"*.

To Lieutenant Rayburn D. Lancaster, strafing the flying boats was like "running the hurdles at a track meet." Lancaster, a native of Stephenville, Texas left two seaplanes burning in his wake. Lieutenants Herbert W. Andridge and Frank "Spot" Collins spotted one trying to take off and shot him down into the sea, then hit three more sitting ducks.

After passing over the seaplane anchorage the Group strafed four escort vessels in the outer harbor. Totals for the mission were twelve enemy seaplanes destroyed, with six more left burning and probably lost, and hits on the four surface ships.

Other pilots on the strafing part of the mission were Flight Officer Bill Slattery, Lieutenant Chuck Steffler, Flight Officer Mark Boone, Lieutenant Ken Rusher, Flight Officer Al Moon. and Bob Baseler's wing man Lieutenant James H. "Available" Jones.

Captain "Herky" Green and his 317th Squadron were flying top cover which gave them a ringside seat, since there was no aerial opposition. They could easily see, as "Herky" summed it up, *"Down below I saw*

These were the pilots involved in the raid on the Italian seaplane base on 1 June 1943. (Front Row) Captain Lancaster, Lieutenant Rusher, Lieutenant Parent, Lieutenant Slattery, Flight Officer Leninger, Flight Officer Boone. (Back Row) Lieutenant Moon, Lieutenant Steffler, Flight Officer Maret, Lieutenant Jones, Major Baseler, Captain Andridge, Lieutenant Collins and Major Garret. (J. W. Cannon)

GERONIMO was flown by Lieutenant Henry H. Brundydge of the 317th Squadron. He scored three kills flying this Warhawk, two Bf 109s and a Macchi 202. (via Dwayne Tabatt)

fire after fire spring up, just as if someone was lighting bonfires. There were also some bonfires caused by the boats that the boys hit on the way out."

No mission is without danger and the P-40 flown by Lieutenant Thomas B. Johnson was hit by anti-aircraft fire and exploded, killing the pilot instantly.

We Gain Notoriety - Hugh Floyd

My recollection was that Axis Sally was the first person to call us the Checkertail Clan.

It was during the North African campaign. I was the "mailman" for the 317th and buddies with another soldier who manned the switch board at night. To keep awake, he listened to the radio and of course the best station featured Axis Sally.

He kept me informed of the latest news and sitting in my primitive "mail room" (tent to most), we used to have a lot of belly laughs at her stories which he repeated to me. I especially recall when a reporter from a Chicago newspaper described her as the "girl with the bed room voice" which was a new term to me but seemed very appropriate in this case.

The incident that drew her attention to us was the mission in which we shot down more than twenty Nazi airplanes which incidentally earned us our first Distinguished Unit Citation. She was on the air that night describing us as Checkertail Butchers plus lots of other uncomplimentary names. She ended up with, ''We will remember you boys in that old Checkertail Clan." That, to the best of my knowledge, was the first time that we were ever referred to as the Checkertail Clan, which now is how we are recognized far and wide.

Lady Eve IV was flown by an unknown pilot of the 319th Fighter Squadron, 325th Fighter Group who scored at least two kills while at Mateur during 1943. (via Dwayne Tabatt)

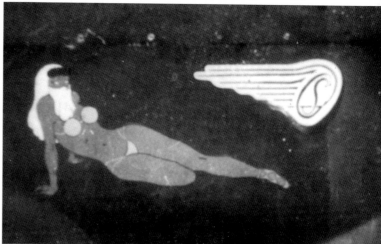

This P-40F was believed to have been flown by Lieutenant Chuck Steffler. The dancing girl on the cowling would probably not have been very popular with the local Muslims. (via Dwayne Tabatt)

Strafing Attack - Bill Lott

Much later, as the war started to wind down in North Africa opposition in our area started to slacken, and we probably suffered some let down in our vigilance. Although this was a normal letdown from the highly keyed up state that we had been in for many months, unfortunately this can and did lead to problems.

One Sunday morning, four of us were scheduled for a dawn fighter sweep, so, as the sun peered above the horizon, our flight was starting

Captain Bunn Hearn, squadron operations officer, flew this P-40F Warhawk named THE STAR OF ALTOONA while the group was based at Mateur Field, Bizerte, Tunisia. Captain Hearn shot down a Bf 109 on the first mission flown from Mateur on 24 June 1943. The mission was a diversionary fighter sweep over Cape Spartivento in southern Sardinia. The aircraft carried a White star marking on the wheel covers. (via Dwayne Tabatt)

EVELYN had an unusual design painted on the wheel covers. The offset circles must have made and interesting effect when the aircraft was taxiing. (Dwayne Tabatt)

its prowl to see if we could find any targets of opportunity. Joe Bloomer was leading the flight with Ted Walton flying his wing and I was leading the element with Archie McKeithen on my wing. We climbed to between eight and ten thousand feet and cruised on a generally easterly course toward Tunis.

After awhile we probably became somewhat complacent as we found nothing on the ground, the sea, or in the air. This was almost our undoing. Abruptly with a deafening roar, blinding explosions completely surrounded us as we came under attack from enemy anti-aircraft guns, probably 88s. Walton and McKeithen were blown out of the air by the first bursts and both Joe and I were flung upside down from which we split-essed to escape the deadly accurate barrage. Walton was never heard of again but McKeithen recovered just above the water and by some miracle brought his crippled bird home.

Captain Ralph G. (Zack) Taylor, Jr. and his ground crew pose with his P-40L named DUCHESS of DURHAM IV. At this time Taylor was an ace with six kills. This P-40 was originally assigned to Herky Green who was almost killed flying it on his first mission and quickly switched to aircraft number 11. The crew chief, SGT Jack Evans, added the name My Gal Sal to the starboard side in honor of the girl who later became his wife. (Jack Evans)

JEANIE II was the first P-40 to carry the 318th Fighter Squadron's Green Dragon insignia on the nose. (via Dwayne Tabatt)

Somehow Joe and I found each other at wave top level, joined up, discovered our birds were still healthy and agreed that retribution was called for. We turned to the east for a few minutes and then with the sun at our backs to blind the foe, we headed for the area that the AA fire came from.

The adrenaline was flowing freely and all we could think of was REVENGE. As we crossed the shoreline below treetop level, seeking the AA guns, a long line of troops materialized in front of us, obviously a morning chow line. Without a spoken word, Joe banked left down the line, and I banked right as we opened fire. It was like shooting ducks in a shooting gallery. We estimated that with each of our six .50 caliber machine guns spitting out some 750 rounds a minute, we had accounted for a minimum of 90 to 100 casualties. In some small measure I guess Walton was avenged, but we still hoped that by some miracle he had survived. Unfortunately, that was not to be and he is now listed as dead.

We did not, however, make the strafing run unscathed. Joe took several hits in his cowling, and I took a .50 caliber slug through the front of my canopy that narrowly missed decapitating me as it exited through the other side of the canopy just behind my head.

Although I have no difficulty recalling the incident, it all comes back with terrifying clarity when I look at the picture we took of Joe sitting on his wing and pointing to all the holes in the side of his bird — and I reflect on how fortunate I am to still be in the land of the living.

Captain Ralph Gordon "Zack" Taylor, Jr.

Taylor was born on 23 December 1913 in Nashville, Tennessee. He moved to Durham, North Carolina and after graduation from high school, entered Duke University. He left Duke early to join the Army Air Corps and get into pilot training. He was awarded his wings in April of 1942 and joined the 66th Fighter Squadron, 57th Fighter Group, flying P-40s. He won the Soldiers Medal for rescuing a fellow pilot from a burning wreck during his stay with the 57th.

"Zack" joined the 325th Group in North Africa as Operations Officer of the 317th Squadron during January of 1943. While leading his squadron in a raid on Sardinian airfields, he was awarded the DFC for shooting down three enemy aircraft to become the first Ace of the Checkertails. He also received the Air Medal with ten Oak Leaf Clusters (OLCs). He added the Legion of Merit to his awards while

serving as the Deputy Wing Commander of the 4th Fighter Wing in Korea during 1950-51. Among his later tours were; commanding officer of the 1st Fighter Wing at Selfridge Field and the 412th Fighter Group, He was the founding father of the Air Force Fighter Center, known as the Tactical Weapons Center at Nellis Air Base during 1966. He retired in 1977 as a Major General.

While with the 325th all of his P-40s were named "Duchess of Durham" with Roman numerals designating each subsequent aircraft. All of his P-40s also carried the individual aircraft number 13. His six victories were all scored on either the 10th or 20th day of the month, two on 10 June, one on 10 July and three on 20 July 1943.

Captain Ralph G. (Zack) Taylor, Jr. points out the name of his P-40L-1-Cu (serial 42-10436), DUCHESS of DURHAM IV. The aircraft carried the number 13 and the name My Gal Sal on the starboard side of the nose. (Jack Evans)

Lieutenant Colonel Austin and his ground crew pose with his P-40, LIGHTHOUSE LOUIE, at Mateur, Tunisia shortly before he was transferred out of the 325th. (Left to Right.) SGT Moring, SGT O'Neal, Colonel Austin and SGT Waller. (G.H. Austin)

The name LIGHTHOUSE LOUIE came from the practice of shooting up light houses on enemy coast lines. The pilots in the group all detected signs that these lighthouses were being used as enemy observation posts and early warning posts. (G.H. Austin)

Captain Joe Boomer's P-40 TRIXIE was outfitted with a makeshift fire bomb mounted on the underfuselage rack. The bomb was made from an empty P-40 drop tank with a hand grenade attached to the nose and homemade fins on the rear. The idea was to drop the tank when it was almost empty on an enemy position instead of just jettisoning the empty tank. (William Stolarzcyk)

Captain Joe Boomer in the cockpit of his P-40F Warhawk. The Green Dragon insignia of the 318th Fighter Squadron appeared in the circle in front of TRIXIE. (J. W. Cannon)

TRIXIE with a conventional underfuselage fuel tank on her centerline rack. The makeshift fire bomb that the group developed was much larger than the standard fuel tank. (J.W. Cannon)

This makeshift fire bomb actually worked and Captain Watkins sent data on it to his father who worked at Eglin Field in the ordnance development section. He later learned that they already had a similar project in the works -- which turned out to be the deadly napalm bomb. (Checkertail Clan)

Seven Hours A Prisoner — John F. Rauth

I took off at 0600 on Friday, 23 July 1943 for a fighter escort mission to a small island off the coast of Sicily. After the fighters we were escorting dropped their bombs, our top cover flight went down to strafe radio installations and targets of opportunity along the coast. We hit the radio installations, a small boat and a lighthouse and, as we left, we sighted two speed boats about five miles offshore. My section leader and his wing man went down on the two boats first, and then my wing man and I strafed them.

Just as I passed over the boat, I caught the smell of coolant and immediately my engine temperature started to rise. I climbed to about 800 feet and throttled back to see if I could cool the engine off, but nothing worked and the temperature continued above the red line with the engine losing power. As I was already below 700 feet, I quickly decided to bail out. I went over the right side and under the horizontal stabilizer. As soon as I was clear of the aircraft, I opened the parachute and almost immediately entered the water. In that brief span I noticed that my airplane had hit the water before my parachute opened.

I struggled trying to get out of the 'chute but the wind was quite brisk, and I was dragged like a surfboard for quite a distance. I was lucky to keep my head above water most of the time, otherwise I probably would have drowned. Finally, I was able to spill the 'chute and in doing so I became entangled in the shroud lines. My Mae West, however, kept me afloat and I was able to cut the shroud lines with my pocket knife to get free. I immediately inflated my dinghy, but had

Lieutenant Colonel Bob Baseler pins full Colonel Eagles on Gordon Auston. His promotion became effective on 28 July 1943, just before he took command of the 319th Bombardment Group. (John C. A. Watkins)

some difficulty in the high wind. It upset at least once, and I was in the water about fifteen minutes before I finally succeeded in getting into the dinghy — it was now about 0720.

I began planning what I would do and initially decided I would paddle to a lighthouse which I saw about three miles away. But then I decided to stay adrift at sea until dark so I could come ashore and hide until the Americans took the island. My only concern at the moment was the high wind which I estimate was blowing me parallel to the shore at about fifteen miles per hour.

Above me, my roommate from flight school, Flight officer Bill Slattery of Birmingham, Alabama, was circling, which gave me a great feeling of comfort. But then he came down low over the water firing his guns. This startled me, and I turned to see that he was firing in front of an approaching fishing boat. I wasn't sure whether I wanted him to keep the boat away from me or not, but it did not matter as I could do nothing about it. As he told me later, he wanted to keep the boat away because Air Rescue was on its way. When his gas ran low, he had to leave and the fishing boat moved in and picked me up. There were six fishermen in the boat and the time was now about 0900.

The fishermen, Italians, seemed very glad to see that I was alive and not hurt. They hugged and kissed me like a long lost brother. They had some dry trousers and some melon which they gave me. Then we started back to shore rowing against the wind. As we neared the shore, I could see that several P-40s were searching off-shore for me. By then it was 1130. Italian soldiers on the coast made us bring the boat into a little quay where they wanted me to surrender since they had seen me bail out of the plane.

(Left to Right) John C.A. Watkins, James F. Garrett, Everett B. Howe, Ralph G. Taylor and Gordon C. Austin pose by one of the group P-40s during the early days of the North African Campaign. (John C. A. Watkins)

There was a young lad in the boat who explained that he would try to surrender himself as the American pilot, hopefully giving me an opportunity to escape. Unfortunately, the soldiers quickly detected his ruse and became extremely upset with him. From my hiding place in the boat, I saw them begin to really rough him up and when they took out their bayonets, I was afraid they were going to kill him, so I decided to give myself up. I had on the civilian trousers and rolling up my wet clothes, I crawled up on the rocks at the point of those Italian guns. That was rough and I admit with all those Italian guns pointed at me, I didn't feel too brave. I came out with my hands up and for the first time in my life I was looking down the wrong end of a loaded gun.

A first-aid corporal was in the group and he swabbed my scratches and bruises with some kind of soothing medicant. I was then taken to an Italian farmhouse and given some water. They took away all my personal possessions except my jewelry. I was then put on a motorcycle and driven about eight miles north of Trapani to a command post. It was the CP for the pillboxes they had along the coast. Here they gave me some grapes and Italian hardtack, so hard that I couldn't chew it. After waiting about ten minutes, we got on the motorcycle again and went to a civilian home on the outskirts of Trapani. Why I was taken there, I have never understood. The owner, a man about 80 years old, had spent twenty years of his life in Omaha, Nebraska, 120 miles from my home. His wife gave me some bread and grapes and a glass of wine. I refused to drink the wine because I thought that perhaps they wanted me to get intoxicated so that I would talk freely. After spending about 15 minutes there, I was taken to Italian head-

LONE TIGER of the 317th Fighter Squadron was flown by Major William R. Reed. His uncle, W. N. Reed, was an ace (10.5 kills) with the American Volunteer Group (AVG - Flying Tigers) in China. Bill was the commander of the 317th and had two kills to his credit. (F. Patt)

Flight Officer Cecil O. Dean and his crew chief SGT Wood look over his P-40, SAWTOOTH Apache just before a mission in May of 1943. (Cecil O. Dean)

(Above and Below) SAWTOOTH Apache was badly shot up by enemy ground fire during a low level mission. The flak hole behind the cockpit was large enough that Dean (left) was able to climb in it. (Cecil O. Dean)

Flight Officer Cecil O. Dean was one of the group's original Sergeant Pilots. His P-40, number 17, was named SAWTOOTH Apache, the stallion was in Black on a Red background, the name SAWTOOTH was in Red, with Apache in Black. (Cecil O. Dean)

quarters in the city.

I went to the commandant's office and the interrogation began. The interrogator was a Lieutenant Colonel Costantino Bruno who spoke through an interpreter, Captain DiGiovanni Salvatore. The captain had attended Public School 17 in Brooklyn, N.Y. for seven years. There also were two lieutenants and a major in the room and an armed guard just outside the door.

Everywhere we had gone, soldiers and civilians gathered around gazing with curiosity at probably the first American pilot they had seen. Some thought I was of Italian descent because I had a pretty good North African sun tan.

At the interrogation, the captain told me that my name was German and that my ancestors came from western Germany, which was almost true because my great grandparents all came from Luxembourg. He gave me quite a lecture about coming to fight against my ancestors and to destroy the mother of civilization which gave us art, literature, architecture and music. He stressed Marconi and said we could not fight the war without the inventions of Marconi. He was also upset about our not fighting against the Russians. It seems that all Italians fear Communism

During this period, I neither approved what they said, nor answered any of their questions and more or less tried to ignore what they said or did. They brought in some food for lunch, and while I was eating they carried on a conversation about me. The food was quite good; chicken broth with rice, Italian bread, wine, a little bit of cheese and

SGT Jerry Strauss on the wing of his P-40L, number 83, before the group's checkers were added. The serial number reveals the aircraft was a P-40L-10-CU. (Paul Maret)

Lieutenant James H. Jones flew number 83 and was assigned as Colonel Baseler's wing man. Some said the aircraft's name, Available, came from the fact that Jones was always available for any mission, actually it came from a L'il Abner comic strip character called - Available Jones. (Jerry Strauss)

some kind of jam. I believe that the food I had was for Italian officers only, because I know the rest of their army doesn't eat that well.

After eating, the real interrogation began. They asked me my name, rank and serial number, and a host of other questions which I was not at liberty to answer. I had my pilot's identification and my AGO card. They became quite confused because my pilot's card rated me a Sergeant pilot as of 6 September 1942 and my AGO card rated me a Flight Officer as of 5 December 1942. Finally, I convinced them that my rank was Flight Officer by the dates on the card. I also had my dogtags from which they got my home address and they determined my age from my AGO card. They asked many forbidden questions: where my outfit was, what kind of plane I was flying, if I liked it, the number of my outfit and how many crew members were on my plane. But I ignored these questions or told them that I could not answer then.

They wanted to know if I was married and how many brothers I had and if any of them were in the Army; what my civilian occupation was; how long I had been overseas; if I was tired of fighting the war, and if I was hurt and was I being treated all right. They definitely wanted to be sure that I was treated right.

It became obvious to me that they expected to be prisoners very soon. They asked how we treated Italian prisoners, if they had to work and also if it was true that we were letting the Sicilians go back to civilian life. Of course I didn't know the answers to these questions, except that they would be treated well.

They then became very friendly and confided to me that they expected to be prisoners in a few days. The commandant said that perhaps he would release me shortly. About that time, a messenger came run-

SGT Jerry Strauss and his maintenance crew work on the engine of Available, Lieutenant James H. Jones' P-40. The aircraft had one .50 caliber machine gun removed from each wing to save weight and improve the aircraft's climb and maneuverability. (Jerry Strauss)

ning into the headquarters babbling away in Italian, something about an "alarme." I took it to mean that the Americans were going to shell the city.

So the Colonel, the Major and the Captain took me to an Italian jeep with driver outside the city and up the side of a mountain between Erice and San Marco, north of Milo Aerodrome. On the drive there I

A line-up of P-40s of the 319th Fighter Squadron during the Spring of 1943, before the group markings were applied. Third from left is Colonel Baseler's aircraft, STUD. (Paul Maret)

The lead aircraft in this line-up of P-40s of the 319th Fighter Squadron is I'M RELUCTANT followed by Colonel Baseler's STUD. (Paul Maret)

Captain Joeseph A. Bloomer also named this P-40, side number 61, TRIXIE. Bloomer was the commander of the 318th Fighter Squadron.

A group of pilots relax outside a tent while waiting for a pre-mission briefing at Montesquieu, Algeria. (John C.A. Watkins)

could see field artillery spotter planes flying around spotting targets. Before we got to the CP for the pillboxes on the mountain, our paratroopers and airborne infantry began to shell the gun positions. I probably could have escaped, but I was afraid that I might get caught in a fire fight between the two sides, so I figured that the best thing was to stay in this quarry where the CP was located.

At 1815 the shelling ceased, the Italian admiral had surrendered the city. The enlisted men chucked their rifles into the quarry and the officers destroyed maps and portfolios. They gave me their weapons and field glasses, and said that they were now my prisoners. Meanwhile, I was watching for American troops to enter the city. It seem ages before I saw the first American coming around the mountain road from the east. I had never seen a paratrooper in his jump outfit before, but easily recognized the American flag on his sleeve. I could see them routing out prisoners from gun emplacements, homes and bivouac areas.

The captain asked that I call an American officer and a sergeant to take over the prisoners. He also asked that I tell them that I had been treated well and that they expected like treatment. He even wanted to know if he could put on civilian clothes and go home. That I refused.

I called to the American troops and said, "Hey soldier, I got some prisoners down here for you." He called back and said, "Hold them, I'll be down there in a minute." When they came within a short distance of me they were astonished to find this individual with no insignia, and carrying Italian weapons and field glasses, who claimed

to be an American pilot. I explained what had happened and wanting some souvenirs, I asked if I could retain one pair of field glasses and a gun. The sergeant then told me to stay with them and they would take me to their CP.

We started down the road with the prisoners, and then the paratroopers decided that since they would be going all over town routing out prisoners, they better let me go by myself to the CP. They gave me directions and told me to take an Italian motorcycle. Mounting the motorcycle, we started out, but it was a slow march, as we were challenged every block by the Americans who wanted identification. Finally we reached division headquarters.

I asked to send a message to my outfit and was told the message center would be in operation within the hour. The speed with which the airborne infantry and paratroopers operate really astonished me. They had marched on foot with full equipment from their jump point which was approximately 175 miles away by road, fighting all the way, and they looked as if they could walk another 175 miles. They had the division headquarters and CP set up an hour and a half after the city surrendered. We even had a mess where officers could eat from plates. That night we slept under blankets on the ground. There were no flies or mosquitoes but the ants plagued us the entire night.

The next morning, I tried to arrange for transportation to some air transport base; however, there was none available. A Colonel in the medical section announced that he had found some American and South African airmen in a Fascist military hospital on the side of the mountain. This intrigued me as we had lost several people and I won-

Flight Officer Scott D. Leninger of the 318th Fighter Squadron and his crew chief pose by his P-40 named VIVIAN.

The group chaplin, Roy Terry, and his assistant help out by digging a slit trench during the Spring of 1943. Such trenches were used as shelters in the event of an air raid. (John C.A. Watkins)

SGT Leo Lorbiecki was the crew chief on P-40 number 57. The crew chief was responsible for the maintenance of the aircraft and had a number of other technicians working for him.

Captain John C. A. Watkins flew to Gibraltar to seek news of his brother, Flight Officer William Watkins who had been declared missing on a ferry flight from England in a P-39. William was forced to make a belly landing on a Spanish beach and was interned by Spanish authorities. (John C. A. Watkins)

Captain John C. A. Watkins and his crew chief pose with his P-40 at Mateur, Tunisia. Watkins had the outboard .50 caliber machine guns removed from each wing to lessen the weight and improve his rate of climb. At this time he was credited with three kills, two German and one Italian. (John C. A. Watkins)

dered if they might be up there. I managed to get transportation there and sure enough found one of the two Lieutenants who were downed on "D" day. He seemed very happy to be alive. There were other Americans and they all were quite thankful for the treatment they had received and happy because the Americans had finally come.

The next morning Captain Reed, who had been shot down on the 10 July, and I started hitch-hiking our way back to an air base. On the road to Sciacca, we drove through very rough mountains. We saw where strategic bridges had been destroyed and found the road full of tank traps. It was a perilous trip.

Further on, toward Licata, we found more destroyed bridges and many more tank traps. At one location, a little railroad town, we found that the place had been completely destroyed by bombs. Several sidings and two trains, one carrying gasoline, had been hit and burned. The railroad tracks were sticking up in the air like spaghetti.

The trip back to North Africa was uneventful. At our first stop, we met a member of the 325th who told us the group had celebrated their 100th day in combat, had flown 100 missions and destroyed 100 enemy planes. Believe me, we were sure glad to be home even if it was only to Africa!!

After his forced landing in Spain, William Watkins was able to escape and make his way to Africa where he joined the 325th with his brother. He was killed on Christmas Eve when his aircraft flew into a mountain in bad weather.

This Warhawk, number 45, flown by Flight Officer Paul M. Hesler, was hit by ground fire during a mission. There are at least ten holes around the cockpit area and a large hole in the flap area; however, none hit the pilot or any vital aircraft systems. The aircraft was repaired and put back into service. (via Dwayne Tabatt)

Captain Harold H. Crossley

Captain Harold H. Crossley was leading his flight on a fighter sweep on 7 September 1943 when he spotted a big sea going tug towing four

(Above and Below) On 3 July 1943, Lieutenant Keith Bryant pulled up sharply in front of this P-40 after a strafing run on a radar installation at Pula, Sardinia. He was killed when the tail of his P-40 was cut off and he crashed. This P-40 was forced to crash land due to damage to the hydraulics from the collision. (John C. A. Watkins)

Captain Joe Bloomer looks at the damage to TRIXIE after a rough mission and reflects on his close call. The object in front of the windscreen is a ring gun sight, which was retained on the P-40 even though the aircraft was outfitted with a much better reflector type gun sight. (J. W. Cannon)

A P-40L of the 317th Fighter Squadron heads out on another mission. The desert camouflage consisted of Sand and Dark Earth over Azure Blue, (via George J. Letzter)

A flight of P-40 Warhawks of the 319th Fighter Squadron over North Africa. Aircraft number 77 was flown by the squadron commander, Captian Walter V. Radovich. (George J. Letzter)

Flight Officer Paul Maret and his crew chief pose with his P-40, number 96, named MYRTLE III. He used .50 caliber shells and bomb symbols as a scoreboard of the dive bombing and strafing missions he flew. Paul was assigned to the 319th Fighter Squadron. (Paul Maret)

barges on a course parallel to the coast line. "Red" was flying his last mission before going home but couldn't pass up such an easy target. He led his flight down in a line astern attack and flew down the length of the string of barges and up to the tug. They roared over the line with all guns blazing away.

"All of a sudden, I heard a noise like things banging on a tin roof and I smelled gun powder. Then I realized in a flash that those barges had targets on them and that the tug was towing them along to give the coastal batteries practice. Boy were we in a spot ! They were shooting

STUD was not used operationally in this special paint scheme, but Colonel Baseler did fly the aircraft to visit other groups and bases. It was sure to cause a stir where ever he went. (R. L. Baseler)

Captain Frank J. Collins (left) and Colonel Baseler in the living quarters area of Mateur field in Tunisia. Spot Collins was an ace with the 319th Fighter Squadron and served as its commander. He scored five kills flying P-40s and added four more while flying P-47s. (R. L. Baseler)

everything from 20mm to the big guns, and we had to go and fly right into their sights ! I thought to myself, all right you sap, this is your last mission !" Fortunately, the enemy gunners were just as surprised as the pilots and, after sinking the barges, the flight was able to get away and return to base.

When maintenance checked over "Red's" P-40, one look was all it took to realize the aircraft was a write off, not worth anything but the scrap pile. Explosive cannon shells had torn great chunks out of the skin, machine gun slugs had riddled the wings and the cockpit was full of flak holes. It was no small miracle that nothing had touched Crossley.

Captain Robert W. Myers

Captain Robert W. Myers, Commanding Officer of the 319th Squadron, decided to do some experimenting shortly after assuming command. He wanted to prove that a P-40 could successfully take off carrying a thousand pound bomb and finally took off with one clinging to the centerline

Bob Baseler in his P-40 STUD in flight over North Africa. This highly colorful P-40 was overall Flat Black with Red ailerons, fuselage flash and cockpit area. In addition, the national insignia also had a Red surround. The name STUD was in Yellow above an Ace of Spades playing card. (R. L. Baseler)

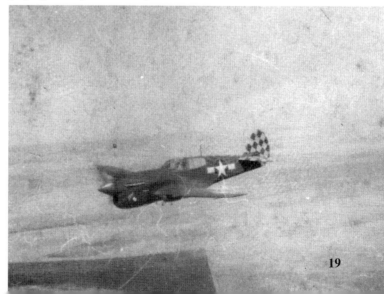

19

Passion Flower III was the group's B-26 hack. It was used to carry critical supplies, VIP, mail and other material. It was also used to give rides to important people, such as Red Cross girls and Army nurses. (Checkertail Clan)

of his ship. Before too long it became more or less a routine thing. The

During the USO show, Frances Langford was asked to pin a Purple Heart medal on Lieutenant William (Bud) Walker. Bob Hope had been tipped off about the location of Walker's wound and made a remark that Miss Langford should kiss it and make it better, which brought down the house. Walker had stopped a piece of flak in his backside. (John C. A. Watkins)

325th was the only Group in the theater to attempt this feat. On 3 September, Major Myers completed his 150th hour of combat flying, at that time it represented a high for the group for the number of hours flown. He completed his tour on 8 September 1943 and left the group.

USO Show

On 10 August 1943, Bob Baseler flew "Passion Flower, 2nd" to El Alouina airport in Tunis to pick up Bob Hope and his USO troupe. Included in the cast were singer Frances Langford, Jack Pepper, Hildegard and Tony Romano. Hope's group was to put on a single performance, have time for lunch plus some extra time to mingle with the troops, roughly about a half day. After lunch in the Group Headquarters mess hall they put on their show on a temporary stage behind the Nissen hut Chapel.

After the performance Miss Langford resplendent in orchid slacks and sweater with a green snood was asked to award some Purple Heart medals to Lieutenant Ronald C. Dove, Flight Officer James I. Poole and Flight Officer Cecil O. Dean. As she presented the award to each they received a big kiss, then Captain Walter B. Walker stepped up for his medal but didn't get the kiss, as it was revealed that he had been wounded in his backside and Hope suggested that she kiss the wounded spot to make it well. Bob's ad lib broke up the audience and had them rolling in the aisles. Walker was embarrassed and confused and the kiss was forgotten in the uproar. He grabbed his medal and made a hasty retreat.

Later on, while chatting with some of the pilots, Frances learned that the inventive genius Captain John Watkins had created a hot shower in a land where there were none. When he and his tent mate Bunn Hearn, the Group Operations Officer, gallantly offered her the exclusive use of "La Douche Supreme" she was determined not to leave until she had enjoyed the luxury of a real shower, one of the comforts of home she had sorely missed. This delay gave Hope a chance to ask Baseler what it was like to fly a bombing mission and one thing led to another and Hope soon found himself in the greenhouse of "Passion Flower 2nd". They took him to a point just south of the bombing line, with some of the pilots flying escort in their P-40s. Bob Baseler had arranged for them to bounce his B-25 and fire their guns for realism. Coupled with the fact that the mission was flown almost at wave top height with an Army Nurse as co-pilot gave Hope a moment to remember.

As a result of all this Hope's group spent the entire day with the 325th and General Headquarters was sending messages wanting to know

Bob Hope once again cracked up Frances Langford when they posed in front of Colonel Baseler's STUD, with a few choice remarks about the meaning of STUD. (Stan Wilson)

Passion Flower 2nd was the group's B-25 hack that gave Bob Hope a wild ride with an Army nurse as his co-pilot. Group P-40s escorted the Mitchell and made mock attacks on it. Members of Hope's troupe pose with the Mitchell after his ride. (Bob Baseler)

Lieutenant Colonel R. L. Baseler with Bob Hope and Frances Langford in front of the Colonel's P-40 named STUD. Baseler started a tradition with this P-40 and later named his P-47, Big Stud and still later, named his P-51, Little Stud. (Ed Doss)

The Bob Hope troupe in the group's bar. Colonel Bob Baseler was seated in the middle, with Bob Hope behind him. Tony Romano (mustache) was on Hope's right and next to him was Frances Langford and Hildegard. (Checkertail Clan)

21

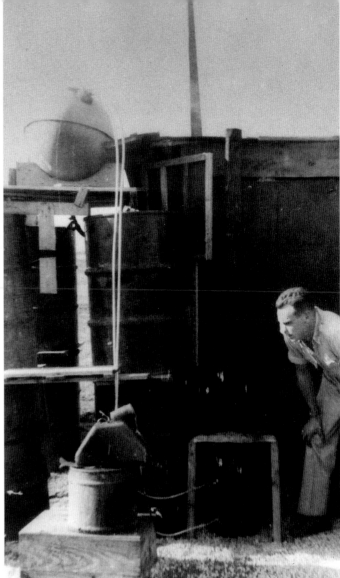

LA DOUCHE SUPREME before the heating system was installed. Engineered by the firm of Watkins and Hearn for the exclusive use of the Lighthouse Boys, it was made famous when a tired Frances Langford used it and lingered in it for so long that the USO troupe was late for its next show. (John C. A. Watkins)

John Watkins proudly displays the fruits of his engineering genius - a working still. He used it to produce a fine wine called Popskull de Tunisie, although others had a number of different names for the brew. (John C. A. Watkins)

Captain Bunn Hearn looks over the water heater which made the shower a more comfortable and luxurious experience. P-40 belly tanks had more than one use in the desert. (John C. A. Watkins)

Bob Hope was not the only USO star to visit the 325th. Colonel Bob Baseler poses with the famous comedian Joe. E. Brown during Brown's visit. Brown's son was a captain in the Army Air Force and was killed in action. As a result, Joe always had a soft spot for Air Force people. (Bob Baseler)

The first enemy aircraft captured by the group was this Bf 109 which they had at Mateur, Tunisia. Jerry Strauss spoke and read German and could translate the placards and instruments. (John C. A. Watkins)

Colonel Baseler had the Bf 109 painted overall Flat Black with the spinner, ailerons, elevators and rudder in Red. In honor of Herr Goering, they named the aircraft Hoimann. Standard USAAF national insignia was carried. (John C. A. Watkins)

Colonel Baseler in the cockpit of the group's captured Bf 109. A few moments later he took off and headed for a P-38 base where he buzzed the chow line in retaliation for the P-38 group's bouncing his P-40s. (John C. A. Watkins)

Later, the group also obtained a captured Fw 190A. The aircraft was ferried in by Jack Senften, then it was immediately grounded by the group commander (Colonel Sluder) who found that the tires were unsafe. Later, while being taxiied, the canopy blew off. (Chet

where the hell Hope and his gang were. Things were eventually smoothed over and when it was time to leave everyone stated that they had an enjoyable time since for most of the men it was the only live American entertainment they had seen since leaving the States.

Hoimann

P-38 pilots felt that anything with a single engine was probably an enemy aircraft and the Checkertails had been bounced any number of times, especially by members of the 14th Fighter Group. The last straw came on a mission when the Lightnings of the 14th were to provide top cover but failed to be there when most needed. It was felt that no doubt they had sighted some enemy aircraft and had gone after them, completely neglecting their primary responsibility. Colonel Baseler shared the feeling when the Clans P-40s returned with more than the usual amount of battle damage. He told his crew to roll out "Hoimann", the Bf 109G that the group had obtained. The Messerschmitt had been painted overall Matte Black, with a Red spinner, rudder, and ailerons. It was also given a set of USAAF insignia and named "Hoimann" in honor of Herr Goering.

Baseler roared off and made a bee line for the P-38 base which was about three miles away. Their field was located at the bottom of a hill and down over this hill roared Bob. He took "Hoimann" across the field at under 100 feet, over the parked P-38s and did a quick pull up to allow them to recognize the intruder's outline. Then roared back across the field on a second pass. It so happened that the group was at chow and standing in the long chow line. When the men recognized the aircraft as a Bf 109 and saw it coming back, the sky was filled with flying Spam, mess kits and other eating utensils as the enlisted men and officers broke for cover in all directions. Bob later recalled the scene as being "like a bunch of chickens after they had seen the shadow of a chicken hawk on the ground". Baseler departed, the area and calmly flew back to base, landed and told his ground crew to put "Hoimann" to bed. He then retired to his quarters. A little later Captain Larry Oldham told Bob that there was a bird colonel there who wanted to see him. Naturally Bob couldn't imagine why anyone would want to see him at that hour, so he went outside and there stood Colonel "Egghead" Garmin, an old buddy from the 94th Pursuit Squadron at Selfridge. Colonel Ralph B. Garmin was now the commander of the 1st Fighter Group and Baseler had buzzed his field, not the 14th's.

Colonel Garmin came directly to the point when Bob asked what brought him over at such an ungodly hour. "Some S.O.B. just buzzed my chow line in a Messerschmitt", he exploded, "It ruined our dinner hour and my men still won't come out of their fox holes. Do you know anything about it ?" "Sure I know all about it" replied Baseler, but said nothing about mistaking his field for the home of the 14th Group. "Why You #*%6+" was all Garmin could mutter. After Baseler explained that he and his men were getting bounced by P-38s and had several cases of

THE BATTLIN BASTARD, aircraft number 5 was assigned to the Headquaters Flight. The aircraft made a belly landing at Mateur after receiving battle damage. (F. Patt)

missing top cover, "Egghead" agreed that he had a valid point and said that he'd get together with the two other P-38 Groups and stress the matter of aircraft identification. There were no more problems after that.

Captain Walter R. Walker, JR.

Walker, a resident of Stamford, Connecticut, was employed in New York City by American Air Lines in a non-flying position when he was drafted into the Army on 12 February 1941. He then applied for admission to the Aviation Cadet Training program and was accepted. He qualified for pilot training during December of 1941, completed pilot training and was commissioned in August of 1942. Granted a leave, he went home and got married in early September. He then was assigned to the 325th. He became an Ace by scoring five quick victories during the month of July, 1943, getting a Bf 109 on the 7 July, another on the 10th and three more on the 30th.

On a fighter sweep over Sardinia his Warhawk took several hits in one of the prop blades causing it to become unbalanced, which resulted in a loss of speed. He dropped out of formation and dove for the deck trying to make himself as inconspicuous as possible. *"Flying alone, well that's different than formation flying where there is strength in numbers. Alone you get the feeling that the bogey man will get you. I kept looking over my shoulder apprehensively because I was a shining mark. The enemy like nothing better than a chance to gang up on a crippled P-40. Suddenly, I saw seven of them coming at me. I began screaming into my radio and asking somebody for God's sake to come back and help me. I really thought my number was up, I kept thinking in best movie style, this is it! The only thing that saved me that day was the tremendous odds against me. They began playing cat and mouse with me and taking no chances as they knew that sooner or later they'd get me."* Suddenly, two P-40s showed up and took on five of the enemy and with only two to shake off, Walker managed to get away.

Walker flew 50 missions getting a DFC, Air Medal with 12 OLC and a Purple Heart. The Purple Heart was awarded after a mission where a 20mm shell tore in his cockpit wounding him in the left hand arm and buttock.

Stan DeCoveny

Stan DeCoveny, a BTO (Big Time Operator), from New York City and some of his friends formed a floating crap game syndicate and in no time at all they had accumulated a sizable amount of cash. Someone suggested that they might be in serious trouble by having so much money and after talking it over they decided they could get rid of it by purchasing a fancy French sports car. They did so with the stipulation that any enlisted man who had the opportunity to get off the base could use it, but that no officers would have the privilege. This was not because of any rank prejudice but simply to prevent any questions being asked about where it had come from. They then decided that they had better get some good insurance coverage just in case, so they took out a policy with a local French insurance company. The policy was in French so they really had no idea what it covered but they at least felt

This deHavilland Moth trainer was used as a squadron hack by the 31st Fighter Squadron. It carried Red stripes on the fin and rudder, which was the group identification markings of the 31st. (George Ording)

safe with it. The arrangement was working well until one day an enlisted man drove it to town, had a few too many drinks but drove back to the base without any problems. As he entered the base he noticed a P-40 just beginning its taxi run and he decided to drag race the P-40. Getting along side of it on the runway, he was actually leading when all of a sudden the car disappeared in a cloud of sand. The poor guy had gone over the edge of a bomb crater and crunched the car. Fortunately, he wasn't hurt but the car was a real mess. They decided since they had insurance maybe they could collect something on the damage so they filed a claim against their insurer in English. The company finally replied, but it was in French. After an exchange of several letters in English and replies in French they got mad and wrote another one in English advising the insurance company that they were going to turn the matter over to the American Provost Marshall and that he would take action on their behalf. Before another reply (in French) could arrive they were shipped out thus putting an end to the affair. Naturally, they had no intention of getting involved with the Provost Marshall so they just charged it off to experience.

P-40 Era Summary

The 325ths record while flying the P-40 was an outstanding one. It consisted of 128 missions, 3,990 sorties, 10,121.45 combat hours, 135 victories, thirty-five losses and 328,820 pounds of bombs dropped. The P-40 era produced four Aces; Lieutenant Colonel Robert L. Baseler, Lieutenant Frank Collins, Captain Walter B. Walker, Jr. and Captain Ralph G. Taylor, Jr.. Four other pilots had four victories and twelve others had three. Sixty-three pilots scored one or more victories in the Warhawk. Enemy aircraft downed included ninety-six Bf 109s, twenty-six Macchi M.C.202s, seven Me 323s, three Ju.52s, and three Fiesler Fi-156s.

The kills were scored while flying a variety of missions. Forty-two were destroyed during escort missions, twenty-seven and two thirds while on bombing missions, thirty-one and one sixteenth on strafing sorties and forty-three on fighter sweeps. Losses by mission type included fifteen on escort missions, three on bombing missions, nine on sweeps, and eight during strafing runs. Losses by type were three due to engine failure, seventeen to enemy fighters, six to flak, one to small arms fire, one by hitting high tension wires, two to mid-air collisions and five to unknown causes.

A post war re-assessment changed these figures somewhat, giving the victories as 133 and 4,197 sorties with 43 losses but only twelve of these were known to be combat losses. The Group was credited with 144 probably destroyed enemy aircraft in combat. There were only 175 aborts and the group dropped 357 500 pound bombs, 119 1,000 pound bombs and 2,805 20 pound bombs, in addition, they were given credit for twenty-four enemy aircraft listed as damaged. Of their own losses, twelve were the result of enemy aircraft, six were due to flak, engine trouble accounted for two and there were eleven operational losses. Twelve aircraft failed to return due to unknown causes. The effective sortie/victory ratio was 30.2 to 1, effective sortie/loss ratio 93.3 to 1

Lieutenant Colonel Baseler in the cockpit of one of the P-47s he flew in combat. Bob was very pleased with the Thunderbolt. (R. L. Baseler)

Thunderbolt

The group began transition training in the Republic P-47D Thunderbolt in September of 1943. From 22 September through 31 October, civilian tech reps from Republic arrived at the group to conduct intensive training for both pilots and ground crews on the Thunderbolt. On 11 October 1943, Colonel Baseler buzzed the field at Mateur with a brand new P-47 that he had ferried in from the assembly area at Bizerte — the Thunderbolt era had begun.

With the advent of the rainy season, the group transferred to Soliman, Tunisia. During their stay there, the group was given the honor of providing escort to the Presidential party on their way to the Teheran Conference.

On 3 November, an advance party departed for Italy to pave the way for the transfer of the group to their new base on the Italian mainland. Between 1 and 3 December, the ground echelon broke camp and on 9 December Colonel Baseler led the group to their new base at Foggia Main. Thanks to bad weather, it would be several days before all the Thunderbolts were ferried into the base, with the last aircraft arriving in the afternoon of 11 December. Another move came on 30 December, when the group moved to Foggia One. Here the routine of missions began in earnest.

When Colonel Baseler returned to the States, he managed to obtain the use of this P-47 which he had painted in 325th markings. He used the aircraft to fly to various War Bond meetings around the country. (R. L. Baseler)

Colonel Baseler in the cockpit of Big STUD in Italy. His sixth victory was scored on 30 January 1944. The windscreen of his Thunderbolt was badly weathered with the bare metal showing through. (R.L. Baseler)

Major Frank J. "Spot" Collins

Collins, a native of Breckenridge, Texas, was an All Conference guard at Texas Wesleyan College. He was in the Texas National Guard during 1934 but his active service did not begin until he became a Cadet in 1942. He graduated from pilot training and joined the 325th. He shot down the first enemy aircraft credited to the Checkertails on 6 May 1943.

During his tour he flew eighty-two combat missions including twenty-seven flown on consecutive days. Five of his victories were scored with the P-40 and four were gained with the P-47. Both of his aircraft carried the name "Lulu" and the individual aircraft number 79. He also was credited with one enemy aircraft damaged and one probable. He commanded the 319th Squadron from 11 March to 20 March 1944. During his tour he was awarded a Silver Star, DFC, and Air Medal with twenty-one Oak Leaf clusters.

After returning to the States he eventually was given command of a P-47 squadron in the Pacific and after flying a few missions over the Kyushu Islands he was blown out of the air by an explosion on the ship he was strafing He was finally picked up by the Japanese after spending two days in the sea and spent the rest of the war as a prisoner of war (POW).

He was deputy commander of the 86th Fighter-Bomber Group at Neubiberg Air Base, Germany from 1951 to 1952. A short tour as CO of the 12th Strategic Wing at Bergstrom AFB, Texas was followed by a tour in the Pentagon. He then took command of Edwards AFB, California. This was followed by a stint as the assistant Director of Operations, 5th Air Force at Fuchu, Japan. In 1958, he became Commander of the 21st Tactical Fighter Wing at Misawa Air Base Japan

Bob Baseler later took command of the Aerial Gunnery School at Harlingen Army Air Field. During his time there he had this P-47N Thunderbolt, which he also named Big STUD. (R.L. Baseler)

Lieutenant Colonel Chet Sluder taxies in with his Thunderbolt at Lesina during the Spring of 1944. This aircraft does not have the name, Shimmy, painted on it. This was the second Thunderbolt to carry the number 52. (C. L. Sluder)

This assignment was followed by duties as Senior Advisor for the Ohio ANG at Lockbourne AFB, the 31st TFW at George AFB, Calif., and command of the 366th TFW at Holloman AFB, NM.

Colonel Chester L. Sluder

Colonel Chester L. Sluder was born in San Antonio, Texas and had his first airplane ride at the age of nine. One of his best friends in the fifth grade was David Lee Hill, who was equally taken with aviation. The two would save their allowances, slip out to Stinson Field to buy dollar rides with Dick Hair, who had been taught to fly by the Stinsons during 1916 in a Wright Model B. David's father was Dr. D. P. Hill, who was the preacher at Chet's family church and also Chaplain of the Texas Rangers. Dave later became known as "Tex" Hill of Flying Tigers fame.

Chet went to the University of Texas in 1932, while on the side he was still taking flying lessons at the Austin airport as often as his money situation permitted. He finally soloed on 12 January 1933 and obtained his solo license (number 28874) on 29 April 1933. At 19 he had a limited local license which authorized him to fly passengers on local flights. His mother became his first passenger, showing her confidence in her young son.

He dropped out of school when he received an appointment as an Aviation Cadet and entered pilot training at Randolph Field on 25 June 1935. He flew the PT-11 in Primary and soloed on 11 July 1935 after only 2:15 hours of dual time. In basic he flew the BT-2 and selected

Shimmy was carried on the nose of this Thunderbolt. This aircraft has the last three number of the serial, 877, painted on the fuselage just forward of the fin in Yellow. The name was in Old English type lettering and was carried just to the rear of the Red cowling band. (C. L. Sluder)

Colonel Sluder with his first P-47D. His first Thunderbolt was a P-47D-11 (serial 42-75011) while his second aircraft was a P-47D-16. The name Shimmy was a contraction of his wife and daughter's names, Zimmy and Sharon. (C.L. Sluder)

Bombardment upon completion of the course, deciding chances were better for a career in that field, although he really wanted Pursuit.. He joined the 61st School Squadron and was assigned to fly the P-12. After flying Keystone bombers, B-3s, B-4s B-5s and B-6s as well as the A-3, 0-19, 0-25, P-1 and P-12 he graduated on 17 June 1936. Upon graduation he was assigned to the 99th Bomb Squadron, 9th Bomb Group, at Mitchell Field, N. Y. still as an Aviation Cadet.

At Mitchell Field he flew the Martin B-10 when not acting as the CO's Bombardier, and was considered an officer, since all members of the crew who were pilots — were officers. Finally, in April of 1937, he wangled a transfer to Langley Field to fly pursuits and joined the 33rd Pursuit Squadron, 8th Pursuit Group, which was equipped with the Curtiss P-6E. His commission as a 2nd Lieutenant came through on 2 June 1937 and with it came orders to Kelly Field to serve as an instructor in the Pursuit Squadron. Before leaving Langley he had managed to get in a week end cross country in his P-6E to Mitchell Field and on the way flew over the hulk of Hindenburg which had crashed and burned the day before. At Kelly some of his students included Boyd D. "Buzz" Wagner (who became the first USAAF ace), Jack Woolams (later a test pilot for Bell Aircraft), Ray Tolliver, Wyatt Exum, Dave Schilling and

General Nathan Twining congratulates Colonel Sluder on receiving the Distinguished Flying Cross. (C.L. Sluder)

Charles M. "Sandy" McCorkle and Bob Baseler.

From Kelly Field Chet was sent first to Brooks Field and then on to Mission, Texas and finally to England to join the 12th Air Force in London where he had the opportunity to fly Spitfires and Hurricanes from Heathrow. Finally he rode a B-17 to North Africa, where he bumped into Bob Baseler who had just taken over the 325th Group. He managed get a thirty day TDY with the 325th and then got a two week extension. During this period he flew twelve P-40 missions and damaged a Bf 109. Upon returning to Headquarters he asked to be permanently assigned to the 325th but since he was senior to Bob Baseler he

Colonel Sluder flew most fighters in the USAAF and USAF prior to his retirement, then he went on to a career in commercial aviation. During 1958, he transitioned to the F-102 Delta Dagger. (C. L. Sluder)

Colonel Sluder's headquarters tent had running water (thanks to a recycled belly tank). The propeller blade on the left read Group Commander and the blade on the right read LT COL Sluder. (C. L. Sluder)

felt that it would not be proper to replace him. He knew Bob was up for promotion, so he went down to the A-I (Personnel) section found Bob's recommendation for promotion, pulled it out of the stack, put it on top and Bob was promoted to Lieutenant Colonel the next day. On the same day he returned to the 325th as Group Exec.

Chet then went to England to collect information on the P-47, since the 325th was the first unit scheduled to get the Thunderbolt in North Africa. While there he paid a visit to the 56th Group and Hub Zempke, whom he knew from the 35th Squadron at Langley. He also saw Gabby Gabreski and Dave Schilling, again two more old friends,

The control tower carried the group checker markings. George Ording recalled that the tower was on the wobbly side and if the wind was blowing from the wrong direction the smoke from the stove would blow back into the tower. (George Ording)

The Checkertail Symphony Orchestra tuning up for a concert of Glenn Miller standards. The band was a good group who provided a lot of good listening pleasure. Moody on violin, Witherspoon on accordion, Blakeslee on trumpet, Wehe on clarinet, Evans played the drums, Furney on bass and Taylor played guitar.

BIG SAM'S SLOP INN had tables for ladies in the rear and featured meat balls and rice as well as SOS on the menu. The inn was a Michelin Five Star resturant and a diners delight.

These maintenance men are constructing a line shack which was made from locally available materials such as drop tank crates. A homemade stove provided both heat and a means to brew coffee. Tables and benches were also made to give the crew a place to play cards while waiting for the return of the group from a mission.

Chet took over command of the Checkertails on 1 April 1944, they flew their last P-47 mission on 24 May and their first P-51 mission an 27 May. Chet flew his last combat mission on 23 August, an escort mission to Markersdorf, Germany. Chet spent time in the Pentagon, with the 10th Tac Recce Wing at Pope AFB, Willaims Field, Arizona, where he transitioned to jets. He was assigned to the Air War College in 1951, then was transferred to Alaska,. He served in the Ohio ANG as Senior Adviser (1953-57), went to Eastern Air Defense Headquarters, served as commander of Thule, Greenland. Was assigned as Commander of the

A line-up of P-47s from the 318th Fighter Squadron prepare for take off on another mission. The Red nose markings were added after the group had been flying P-47s for quite some time. (Checkertail Clan)

Detroit Air Defense Sector, then went to the NORAD Team at SAC and ended his 30 year career as commander of GEEIA Region at Tinker AFB, Oklahoma in 1965.

After retiring he worked for a local air service in Albuquerque where he settled, flying VIPs and scientists to Los Alamos from Albuquerque. During his flying career Colonel Sluder flew twenty different civil aircraft, five that were both civil and military, and sixty-four military types and these figures do not include different models or marks of the same airplane. He has flown every thing from an Aeronca C-3 to the F-106B, and everything from single engine fighters up to four engine bombers.

Herky Green

Colonel Herschel (Herky) H. Green, who commanded the 317th Fighter Squadron in the 325th Fighter Group was a triple ace whose introduction to the combat area came about in a novel way — he took off from an aircraft carrier.

This would not be unusual for a Navy pilot, but Herky was in the Army Air Corps and was flying a P-40 Warhawk. Even though it was many years ago, the experience is still vivid in his mind. He went on to rack up eighteen victories while flying 100 combat missions during two and a half years in North Africa and Italy. He also participated in the first "shuttle" mission to Russia.

But his story begins in December of 1942 when he was a member of the 317th Fighter Squadron of the 325th Fighter Group at Providence, R.I. At the time he had a detachment of six P-40s in East Boston. "I

These pilots were involved in a mission to Villaorba on 30 January 1944 in which the 325th destroyed a total of thirty-eight enemy aircraft and damaged another six. Herky Green was credited with six kills on this mission. (Left to Right- standing) Herky Green, Gene Emmons, Bill Chick, J.C. Doerty, George Novotny, John L. Brower and Gerry Edwards. (Sitting) unidentified, Cecil Dean, Walt Walker, Edsel Paulk and Neil Carrol. Seven out of this group were aces. (Richard M. Hill)

This P-47D of the 317th Fighter Squadron was shot up by ground fire, but was able to make it back to base in spite of severe damage to the tail. (Checkertail Clan)

Number 87 of the 319th Fighter Squadron lost a portion of its right wing and suffered damage to its left wing as well. A lifting bar inserted through the rear fuselage allows the maintenance crew to lift the aircraft. (Checkertail Clan)

This Thunderbolt crashed on takeoff and burned. The pilot was able to escape without serious injury. (Checkertail Clan)

suppose at the time I was the air defender of Boston," he grinned, "ludicrous as it now seems."

Then came orders moving the group to Langley Field, Va. where it began practicing carrier-type takeoffs on an area marked out on the runway — with no real hint of what was to come.

That is most of the pilots practiced the takeoffs and landings, Colonel Green recalled, explaining that, *"I was always busy doing something else and never got the chance."* Following a few days at Langley, the outfit packed up again, flew to a nearby Navy field and then actually taxied the aircraft down city streets to the dock where the P-40s were hoisted aboard the aircraft carrier USS RANGER. The orders under which the group was moving were dated 1 January 1943 and were *"quite interesting in that everything pertinent had been left blank."* *"The whole affair,"* Colonel Green chuckled, *"was right out of Arch Whitehouse, even to the sealed orders which were opened only when we were at sea. We then learned we were going to North Africa which wasn't hard to guess at this time, and that we were going to take off from the carrier, which also wasn't hard to guess."*

During most of the voyage, the Army Air Corps pilots were "treated" to movies on carrier operations, *"probably in an attempt to teach us*

something."

"Unfortunately, however, the Navy appeared interested only in those films which depicted the use of incorrect techniques, so we spent hours watching aircraft spin, crash and burn — and get pushed off the carrier. This, as you can imagine, did little to ease our minds."

But for the most part the entire group of seventy-five P-40s took off from the carrier without serious incident, although Colonel Green did have a few anxious moments. He recalled that he "hoisted" his P-40 into the air much before he should have thinking that he had run out of deck. Then while he was settling toward the water in a semi-stalled con-

Few aces scored six victories on a single mission. Captain Herky Green, who commanded the 317th Fighter Squadron, accomplished this while flying a borrowed aircraft! His normal P-47, number 11, was down for repairs so he borrowed Captain Bunn Hearns aircraft, The Star of Altoona. Green broke off the engagement after downing his sixth enemy aircraft because he saw tracers, which was a group sign that he was down to fifty rounds of ammunition per gun. He did not know it, but Hearns carried 800 rounds per gun, instead of the normal group practice of carrying only 400 rounds. Had he known this, his tally for the mission might have been even higher. (via Dwayne Tabatt)

Aircraft number 54 made an emergency landing after ground fire damaged the flaps and landing gear. Incidents such as this kept the maintenance personnel busy. (Checkertail Clan)

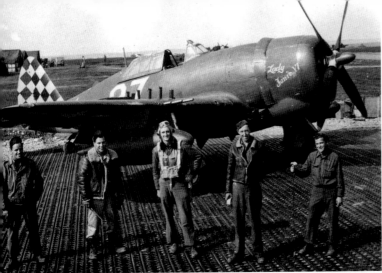

Lieutenant John M. Simmons (center), an ace with the 317th Fighter Squadron who scored a total of seven victories, poses in front of his P-47 with his ground crew (left-right) John Kerr, Pete Vitale, J. Bramer and Ira Grandel. His Thunderbolt carried the name LADY JANIE VI on the starboard side and RUTHLESS RUTHIE on the port side. Simmons was killed after the war in the crash of a T-33 at Eglin AFB. (Ira Grandel)

Barbara May was Lieutenant Donald J. MacDonalds P-47. He was later shot down on a mission to Galati, on 6 June 1944, while flying a P-51.Mustang and became a POW. (D. J. MacDonald)

dition, a flying suit which had been stuffed behind him began creeping out through the open canopy into the slipstream. *"Trying to hang onto that flying suit and keep the plane on an even keel while just inches off the water gave me a few trying moments,"* he admitted, *"but I*

finally got the suit in my lap, closed the canopy and made a "miraculous" recovery."

He and the remainder of the group landed at Casablanca to find that the surprises were not over. *"No one knew we were coming — and that was my introduction to North Africa."*

Herky was born in Mayfield, Ky on 3 July 1920, the only son of Mr. and Mrs. Ted Green. After completing high school he attended Vanderbilt University at Nashville, Tenn where he studied mechanical engineering for two years and also fulfilled a long-time ambition by learning to fly, under a government sponsored program.

In September of 1941, he was appointed a flying cadet in the Army

This Thunderbolt of the 319th Fighter Squadron turned over on landing. The crash crew uses a mobile crane to return the aircraft to its landing gear. Such landing accidents were not uncommon in the rainy season in Italy. The rains often made field conditions extremely poor. (Stan Wilson)

This Thunderbolt from the 318th looks like a beached humpback whale after a rough landing broke its back. The aircraft had been hit by ground fire which weakened the fuselage structure. (Stan Wilson)

ROWDY, number 66, was flown by Lieutenant Sam E. Brown of the 318th Fighter Squadron. His crew chief is painting on his first kill scored on 3 March 1944. Sam added two more during his tour with the Checkertails. (M. Stolarzcyk)

Air Corps and received his pilot wings and commission as a Second Lieutenant one year later at Foster Field, Texas.

His initial assignment to the 57th Fighter Group in Rhode Island was followed shortly by a transfer to the 325th Fighter Group. During his two and half year combat tour with the 325th FG in North Africa and Italy, he served as squadron operations officer, squadron commander and later on the Fifteenth Air Force operations staff. During this period he flew 100 combat missions in the P-40, P-47, and P-51 and was credited with the destruction of eighteen enemy aircraft in the air and ten on the ground. When "promoted" to his desk job, he had the highest number of kills in the Mediterranean Theater.

His wartime exploits earned him the Distinguished Service Cross,

Crew Chief Ed Doss and a friend visit with Nasty Nancy, a 319th Fighter Squadron Thunderbolt. The aircraft number and pilot are unknown. (Checkertail Clan)

Baby Eileen was one of the group's more colorful Thunderbolts, not only did it have a checkertail and Red nose band, it also had checkered cowling flaps and a sharksmouth painted on each drop tank. (Checkertail Clan)

Silver Star, Distinguished Flying Cross with one Oak Leaf Cluster, Purple Heart, Croix de Guerre with Palm and Air Medal with 25 Oak Leaf Clusters.

Wartime experiences still particularly vivid to him were his first combat mission and aerial victory and the mission during which he knocked down six enemy aircraft.

His first crack at the enemy came on 19 May 1943 when his group, then stationed at an airfield near Constantine in North Africa, was escorting a formation of bombers on a raid on the Mediterranean island of Sardinia.

"Just about the time our formation crossed the coast of Sardinia," Colonel Green said, *"we were jumped by enemy fighters and things swiftly developed into a mad melee. Everywhere I turned those jokers were on top of me. The next thing I knew a Bf 109 was coming head-on, firing. The only thing I knew to do was to fly straight at him and fire. I finally hit him before he hit me. We passed just a matter of feet apart. Why I didn't crash into him, I'll never know. I wasn't really rational at the time."* That was his first aerial victory, but his P-40 had been so badly riddled that after landing, it was just wheeled away to the junk yard. That this was also the first and last time that he tempted fate and carried the number "13" on his plane. Although number "13" was subsequently assigned to Wayne Lowry who became a famous ace in his

Lieutenant John R. Booth of Toledo examines the damage to his aircraft on 24 March 1944. His wing was some four feet shorter than when he took off thanks to a collision with a Bf 109. The Messerschemitt then flew into another and they both exploded. On a later mission to Brasov, Romania, he was listed as Missing in Action. (Bob Barkey)

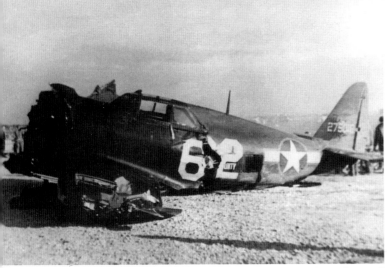

This 318th Fighter Squadron Thunderbolt made a crash landing and was a total loss. (W. Stolarzcyk)

SGT William Stolarczuk of Libby, Montana served as a crew chief with the 318th Squadron. One of his duties was charging the wing guns before the P-47 went out on a mission. The .50 caliber ammunition not only took up a lot of space, but also weighed a lot and some pilots preferred to fly with reduced ammunition loads. (W. Stolarczuk)

Lieutenant William L. Adams flew this Thunderbolt named Butch. He is outfitted with flight coveralls, flight helmet, gloves and standard G.I. issue shoes. Most pilots wore these shoes on missions, since the shoes they normally wore would be lost in the event of a bail out. These shoes, on the other hand, would stay on their feet and were excellent for walking over bad terrain. (William E. Gebhard)

own right.

It was on one of his first missions in the P-47, shortly after his group had transferred to Italy, that he bagged an even half dozen enemy aircraft during a wild forty-five minutes in northern Italy. It occurred on 30 January 1944 during a counter-air strike against targets in northern Italy.

"Our group," he said, *"was to fly up the Adriatic on the deck to*

Number 78 was flown by Lieutenant Stewert E. Myers of the 319th Fighter Squadron. (Checkertail Clan)

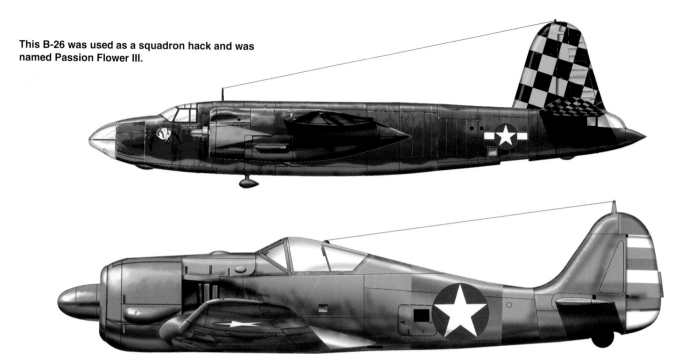

This B-26 was used as a squadron hack and was named Passion Flower III.

This captured Fw 190 was grounded by the group commander, Lieutenant Colonel Chet Sluder, because it had bad tires and was dangerous to fly.

Another captured German fighter was Hoimann, a Bf 109G that was test flown by the group commander, Robert L. Baseler.

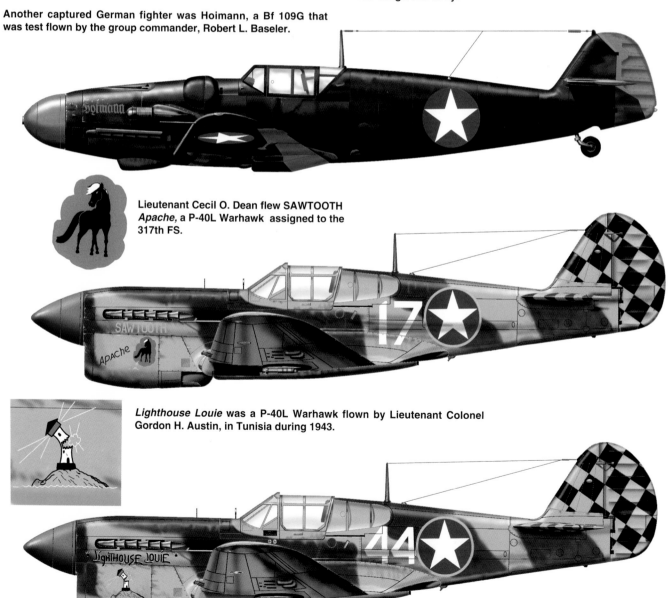

Lieutenant Cecil O. Dean flew SAWTOOTH *Apache,* a P-40L Warhawk assigned to the 317th FS.

Lighthouse Louie was a P-40L Warhawk flown by Lieutenant Colonel Gordon H. Austin, in Tunisia during 1943.

avoid detection, hop over the target area some fifteen minutes before the bombers arrived and keep everything down. When we reached altitude over the target area I spotted about a dozen three-engine Ju 52 transports down low," Colonel Green recalled, going on to say, "I took one flight of four planes, peeled off and went after them."

"When we reached their altitude, about 1,500 feet off the terrain, they were strung out in a long gaggle as if they were spacing themselves to land at one of the several enemy airfields in the area. They were in such a position that I was able to come right through them, firing at first one and then another. I got four on that pass." "I pulled up to make another pass, figuring we could end the war right there, and found them all gone, most falling victim to the other three members of my flight and the rest bellying in to keep from being shot down."

"By this time the planes we had left upstairs were running into opposition and while we were attempting to join them, down would come an enemy plane trying to escape and off we would go after him. This happened several times and, as a matter of fact, we never did get back with the rest of the group." Colonel Green bagged his fifth plane, a Bf 109, in a prolonged tree-top chase and in the process became separated from the rest of his flight so, "I figured this was a good time to head for home." Crossing the Italian coAst near Venice at about 10,000 feet he spotted a Dornier 217 which he swung behind and set afire with a burst into the left engine. He watched it blow up when the pilot attempted to belly it in on the coast —victory number six. On that one mission he and his flight ended up with a total of fifteen victories while the group total came to some thirty-seven enemy aircraft.

While in Italy he also flew fighter cover on the first "shuttle" bombing mission across enemy territory to Russia, landing at a field in the Ukraine. "We flew a couple of missions out of the Russian field," he said, "before heading back to Italy. The next such mission was out of England."

Following the war, Herky had many interesting assignments and accumulated over 4,000 flying hours logging time in the F-80, F-89, F-100, F-101 and F102. He married the former Jeanne Louise Hopewell of Paducah, Ky and the couple have two daughters.

On 1 April 1964, he retired from the Air Force and was employed by Hughes Aircraft Company until his retirement on 10 September 1982.

Captain William A. Rynne

Captain Rynne was a member of the 317th Fighter Squadron but was

(Above and Below) SPIRIT OF MILWAUKEE COUNTY was flown by Lieutenant Paul Dowd, Jr. He and his crew chief were both from Milwaukee, Wisconsin. Dowd was credited with one victory. (Paul Dowd)

Flight Officer Cecil O. Dean's number 17 carried this Black Panther insignia on the side of the cowling. The Panther was Black with Red eyes, lips and nose. The teeth, whiskers and eyeballs were in White. The Bf 109 was Gray Green. (Checkertail Clan)

Lieutenant Dowd later flew a second Thunderbolt that had the name and art work changed. The nose band was now swept back, the beer mug was above and the name was below the Red triangle. (Paul Dowd via Dick Hill)

Don Roberts in the cockpit of Lieutenant Leland J. Stacy Jr.'s Thunderbolt, number 12. The aircraft was assigned to the 317th Fighter Squadron. (Via Jeff Ethell)

later appointed commander of the 319th Squadron. He was an Ace with five victories, all of which were scored while flying a P-47. Initially he flew number 29 named "Ginger", A P-47D (42-75829). His time as CO of the 319th lasted only eight days, assuming command on 20 March, he was hit by flak while leading his squadron on the 28th. Although he bailed out he was badly burned and became a POW. His burns were so severe that when he returned to the States he became pretty much of a recluse and did not attend reunions of the group. The mission on which he was shot down was a penetration support to the marshalling yards at Verona. Lost along with Rynne was A. 0. Jones and Lieutenant Hudson who earlier had accidentally shot down Jimmy Jones. On the same mission, Lieutenant Booth collided with a Bf 109 who in turn collided with his own wingman and both crash, Booth got credit for two 109s destroyed without firing a shot, but he lost several feet of his wing tip. During his tour Rynne was credited with four Bf 109s and a SM-82.

Major Lewis W. "Bill" Chick, Jr.

Bill Chick, a native of Blanco, Texas, arrived in England in January of 1943 and was assigned to the 4th Fighter Group. He had been previously stationed in the Canal Zone flying P-36s and P-40s. Now he found himself flying the Spitfire Mark V in combat, but in April the Group switched to the P-47 and after a brief period he was transferred to Headquarters, 8th Air Force Fighter Command in the Combat Operations Section. Later, he managed to get assigned to the 355th Fighter Group, another Thunderbolt outfit, to resume combat flying. In

Little Sir Echo was assigned to the 317th Fighter Squadron and was flown by one of the squadron's aces -- Edsel Paulk. The aircraft was named after a popular song of the era. (Stan Wilson)

Lieutenant Chester L. Williamson flew as wingman for Lieutenant Benjamin Emmert. The underwing tanks on this P-47D are actually P-38 drop tanks. The underwing pylon on the Thunderbolt was locally modified to accept these large streamlined tanks, replacing the bulky underfuselage tanks issued with the P-47. (Checkertail Clan)

Although the name has been deleted by wartime censors, this Thunderbolt was Colonel Sluder's Shimmy. It was actually located just forward of the small victory marking (White circle) in front of the windscreen. (C.L. Sluder)

November of 1943 he left England to join the 325th in Italy to help them get the best from their P-47s. He arrived at Solomon Air Field on Cape Bon on 3 December. After the 325th moved to Foggia Main on 10 December they went to work. Chick was made Squadron Commander of the 317th and got "Herky" Green as his tent mate and Operations Officer. Green at the time was the leading ace of the 15th Air Force.

Major Chicks comments on the P-47 was that, *"The Jug proved to be a good airplane which performed well against anything the Germans had at that time. In addition, it could take a terrific beating and come back for more. Our jugs were all equipped with water injection and the factory word was, 2,800 RPM maximum with 52 inches of mercury manifold pressure dry and 56 inches wet. The 317th set their engines up to allow 70 inches of mercury wet which really gave the old Jug a kick in the pants for a few minutes and drove the factory tech rep nuts.*

Aircraft number 60 was flown by Lt Bill Adams. The individual aircraft number was painted under the cowling lip in White as a matter of standard practice. (Dick Hill)

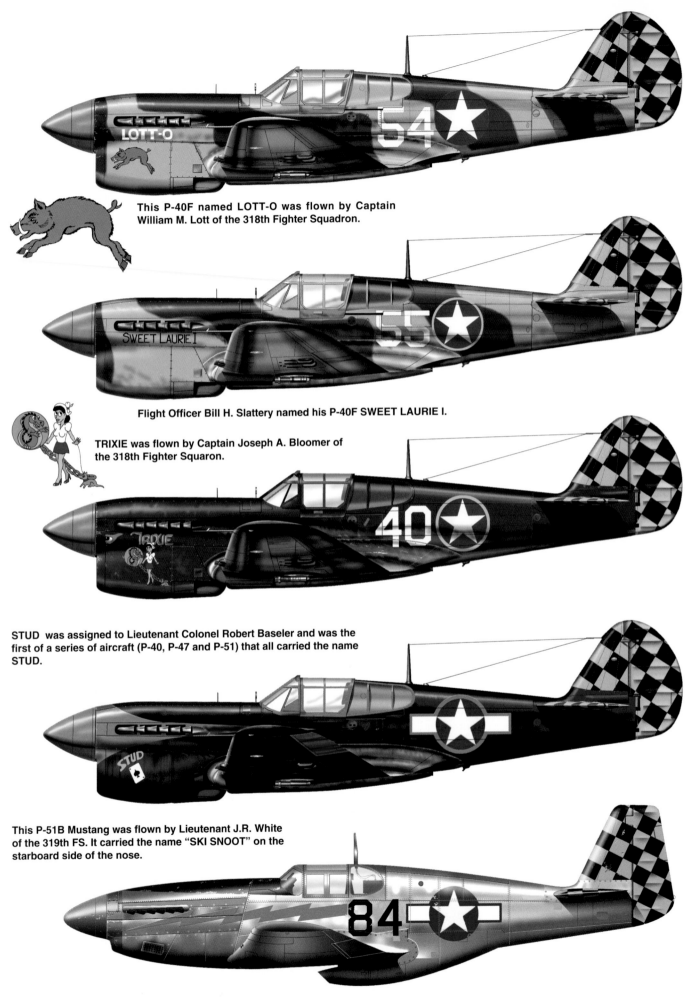

This P-40F named LOTT-O was flown by Captain William M. Lott of the 318th Fighter Squadron.

Flight Officer Bill H. Slattery named his P-40F SWEET LAURIE I.

TRIXIE was flown by Captain Joseph A. Bloomer of the 318th Fighter Squaron.

STUD was assigned to Lieutenant Colonel Robert Baseler and was the first of a series of aircraft (P-40, P-47 and P-51) that all carried the name STUD.

This P-51B Mustang was flown by Lieutenant J.R. White of the 319th FS. It carried the name "SKI SNOOT" on the starboard side of the nose.

Lieutenant Colonel Robert Baseler scored his sixth kill while flying BIG STUD.

This P-47D was flown by Lieutenant Cecil O, Dean of the 317th FS in Italy during 1944.

Lieutenant Sam E. Brown of the 317th Fighter Squadron flew this unnamed P-47D Thunderbolt.

SPIRIT OF DeSOTO COUNTY was flown by Lieutenant Lamar Perry of the 318th Fighter Squadron.

Lieutenant William K. Carswell flew THE JENNY "A", which was named after a Republic Aviation worker.

Rocky was flown by Major Lewis W. (Bill) Chick, Jr. who transferred to the group from the 4th Fighter Group in England. The aircraft has two kill markings under the cockpit. (Checkertail Clan)

Anyway, it worked and we left them that way. With the doctrine I was teaching of turn the airplane gently and maintain an indicated airspeed of at least 250 mph, we could out run anything in the air that could give us trouble in combat. Our evasive action was to dive till you saw 500 mph on the airspeed indicator and you could be sure no one was behind you any longer, since they would have shed their wings by this time. Also, the airplane was faster than anything we would run up against."

After the war Bill was Chief of the USAF Mission to Bolivia in 1949-50 and worked in Lima, Peru as well. In a bar in the hotel there was a bartender with a German accent and during a conversation Bill learned that he had been a fighter pilot. After exchanging experiences they determined that he had been one of the two victories Bill had scored on 30 January 1944, when he shot down two aircraft on a single mission. They became good friends who admired and respected each other.

Bill recalled another amusing incident after the 30 January mission, a P-38 pilot called "Herky" Green to tell him that he had passed him as the leading Ace, since he had gotten two that day and had only been one behind. He was more than surprised when Green mentioned that he had scored six kills that day.

This Thunderbolt had two names, CHERRY MARY appeared on the starboard side and SPIRIT OF DeSOTO COUNTY appeared on the port. The aircraft was assigned to Lieutenant Lamar Perry of the 318th Fighter Squadron. (Paul Dowd via Bill Gebhard)

Major Chick flew with two other groups, the 4th and 355th before joining the 325th. He scored all of his six kills between 14 January and 3 March 1944. He served as squadron commander of the 317th Fighter Squadron and was promoted to Lieutenant Colonel just before his tour with the Checkertails was completed. (Checkertail Clan)

Bill Chick left the 325th on 29 March 1944 after a total of eighty-seven missions and had six confirmed kills (all Bf 109s) and had strafed a ship in a Northern Italian port, which he said was damned near my last mission. This flight took place on 19 December 1943, on the way back from the Innsbruck marshaling yards. He damaged a 200 foot boat at Rozzeto di Abrizi. Bill also recalled that the first 26 days in Italy he never had a bath and that it was possible that during that period a small piece of flak embedded itself in his leg.

Thunderbolt Commentary

The P-47 Thunderbolt was called the "Jug" and was well liked by just about all of the pilots:

Bob Baseler commented on the P-47:

"The first time I tried my D-10, I climbed from a standing start to 30,000 feet in 10 minutes. I guess I used about 250 gallons of gas doing it, and this was without water, just standard military power 52 inches of mercury and 2,700 RPMs. I and my crew chief double-ought sandpapered my airplane and it increased my top speed 15 mph at 1,000 feet. Joe Parker, Republic's chief test pilot told me that was about what to expect as they had tried it at Farmingdale with the same results."

"Due to those monstrosities (wing tank pylons) they used on it, my P-47D-16 was exactly 50 mph slower with the same throttle setting, 52 inches of mercury and 2,700 RPMs than without the tanks. Colonel Claire Baunche who was director of Operational Engineering in XII Bomber Command, under General Jimmy Doolittle had Joe Parker get him the stress analysis for that part of the wing and he redesigned the pylon — put a buffer plate on it and used two P-38 pylons. Now

the airplane slowed down less than one mile per hour!"

"Joe Parker told me, if you tangle with an Fw 190 or Bf 109 at 25,000 feet and want to beat him to 30,000 then dive to 20,000 and zoom and you'll be waiting for him up there. It was really true, the Jug's zoom qualities were tremendous. I used to have 2,300 RPM and 32-33 inches of manifold pressure, when I was leading a group of forty-eight P-47s, in order to allow the last man in formation to maneuver at all." I feel that I'm speaking for the entire Group when I say we liked the P-47 very well. It was a fine weapon, could take lots of punishment and dish it out, too. It was dependable, no worrying about coolant leaks, easy to maintain, and just an all round good aircraft."

Number 49 of the 318th Squadron flipped over after hitting a hole in the runway. This type of accident was common in the muddy field conditions in Italy.

Chet Sluder

"When we got the Jugs I insisted that we eliminate tracers and depend on the 100-mil sight with which the Jug was equipped. A lot of the "old sports" from Africa grumbled, but our results in the Jug certainly justified the change. Many, many times our gun cameras showed that a Jerry didn't know he was being shot at until he was hit, and then it was too late for him to do much about it. Fifty rounds from the end of the belt we had five rounds of tracers as a warning to the pilot that he was about out of ammo."

Colonel Sluder had a few negative comments on the P-47 as it came from the factory. "Right in front of the pilot's nose was a placard on the instrument panel which read "Drop external tanks from level flight at a speed not exceeding 160 IAS. Ridiculous! Can you imagine a pilot having a mess of Messerschmitts bounce him out of the sun slowing down to 160, carefully leveling off his aircraft and then pulling his tank release? On the contrary, it was not unusual to see a pair of drop tanks suspended in mid-air, left there by an edgy pilot who jerked his tanks and went into a hard break, all at the same time."

"Another example: On the floor of the Jug was the fuel selector switch by which you selected internal and external fuel. When your wing tanks went dry you reached down to the floor and switched to internal. The idiocy of such an arrangement was brought home to me when we flew the Big Deal up the middle of the Adriatic — all aircraft were on the deck. It was an interesting exercise when it came time to switch tanks. I had to get the airplane trimmed real good, duck down to the floor, switch tanks, hoping that I didn't leave the selector off the detent in my hurry. and get my head up again before I hit the water or gained altitude. I'm sure that Bob Baseler with his eight foot arms didn't have any trouble, but my arms are in proportion to my 5 foot 6 inch height. Someone in the outfit came up with a U-shaped tube on the fuel selector which made it possible for even me to reach the handle." Chet would have been even more worried over switching tanks if he had known that Baseler had instructed his "Tail End Charlie" to shoot down any plane that exceeded the set altitude by more than fifty feet.

Wayne Lowry

"The Thunderbolt turned out to be a lovable beast, forgiving my many errors of omission as well as of commission. Even though some of my manipulations, in effect, pushed the spin, crash and burn button she simply refused to die and seemed to be telling me, "I don't care about you, you damned fool, but I'm going to live". Performance wise, in a turn the Jug was nothing to shout about, but at high altitude it had the most amazing maneuverability of any airplane I have ever flown. She seemed to thrive on thin air. I can also say that I have never flown an aircraft before or since that could get rid of so much altitude in such a short time. It also had an inclination to reverse its controls in a high speed dive, especially in the thin air at higher altitudes."

Six Aces were produced while flying the P-47. Major "Herky" Green

Salvage crews use several mobile cranes to right number 49 and place it back on its landing gear. Once the aircraft was righted, it could be towed back to the squadron area for a detailed assessment of the damage. (William Stolarczyk)

was high with ten kills, Lieutenant Gene Emmons had nine, Bill Chick was credited with six and Captain Rynne, Lieutenant Paulk and Lieutenant Novotny all had five victories.

The 325th flew 97 missions with the P-47, a total of 3,626 sorties and 15,280 combat hours. They shot down 101 Bf 109s, twelve Fw 190s, ten M.C.202s, five M.C.205s, 3 S.M.82s, two G.55s, two Me 4l0s, two Ju.88's, and one each Me-110, Re 2001, Do.217, Hs l26, and Fi 156, for a total of 153 kills. The 325th suffered only thirty-eight losses. Eighteen of these losses occurred on route cover missions, eight on withdrawal cover, six on penetration support and only six on fighter

The major structural damage to Thunderbolt number 49 appears to be the loss of the upper fin and rudder. It was felt that the aircraft was repairable and eventually it returned to service. (William Stolarczsyk)

The SPIRIT OF **MILWAUKEE** COUNTY was the mount of Lieutenant Paul B. Dowd of the 318th FS.

Topper of the 317th FS was flown by Lieutenant Warren F. Penny.

Lieutenant Penny also flew the only Natural Metal P-47 assigned to the group, which he also named *Topper*.

Rocky was the Thunderbolt assigned to Major Lewis W. "Bill" Chick, Jr. of the 317th FS.

Although it was not carried on the aircraft, Captain Frank J. Collins called his aircraft Lulu.

Lieutenant Richard S. Deakins, an ace with five kills, flew this P-51B.

Penrod was flown by Captain Roy B. Hogg, an Ace with six kills. Most group Mustangs had the last three digits of the serial painted on the rear fuselage in Black.

This P-51B, named SHIMMY III, was flown by the Group Commander, Lieutenant Colonel Chester L. Sluder

This P-47D Thunderbolt was named *Ruthless Ruthie* by its pilot, Lieutenant George P. Novotny of the 317th FS.

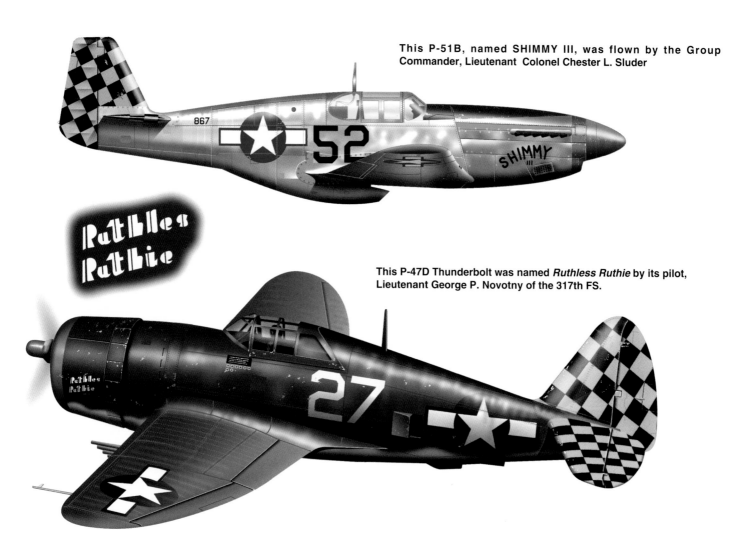

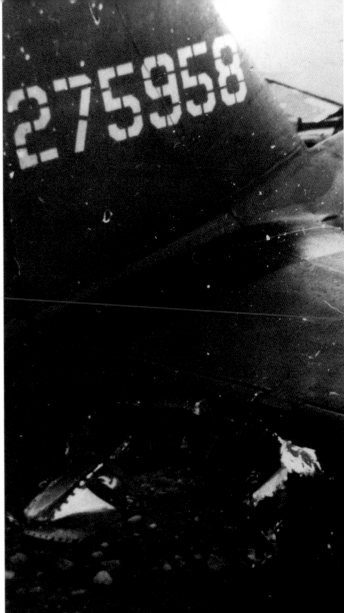

(Above and Left) Butch, number fifty of the 318th Fighter Squadron was assigned to Lieutenant L. W. Adams and crewed by SGT William Stolarczyk. The aircraft was shot up by an enemy fighter on a mission and had large pieces shot out of the wing, starboard elevator, and port horizontal sta-bilizer/elevator. Much of the damage was actually minor in nature, being mostly sheet metal work with little internal dam-age. This sequence proves the ruggedness of the Thunderbolt. The P-47 had a well deserved reputation of being able to with-stand a lot of battle damage and still get its pilot home. (William Stolarczyk)

TOPPER, number 30, was assigned to the 317th Fighter Squaron and flown by Lieutenant Warren F. Penny. The Olive Drab and Neutral Gray Thunderbolt carried the serial 42-75007. (Checkertail Clan)

sweeps. Causes of these losses were: nine to enemy aircraft, eight due to weather, five were hit by flak, eleven for reasons unknown, four were lost for other causes and only one due to mechanical failure.

Victories occurred on the following mission types, thirty on missions against lines of communication, 101 in counter-air or escort operations and twenty-two against towns and industries. Missions flown included: escort 3,449 sorties with 332 aborts, fighter sweeps 979 sorties with 72 aborts.

Lieutenant Penny had a second Thunderbolt also named TOPPER. This aircraft was unusual in that it is believed that it was the only overall Natural Metal Thunderbolt in the group. At this time, March of 1944, the group was based in San Pancrazio, Italy. (via James V. Crow)

TOPPER ran into some trouble on landing at San Pancrario, Italy and damaged the landing gear. The damage was not extensive and the aircraft was repaired and put back into service. (James V. Crow)

Lieutenant Richard S. Deakins of the 318th Fighter Squadron was an ace with five kills and one damaged to his credit. He scored two kills with the P-47 and the rest with the P-51. His Thunderbolt was number 63 (serial 42-75824). While flying number 65, a squadron hack, he flew into the side of a mountain and was killed. (Cannon)

Italian fighter pilots of the 51st Stormo look over a Thunderbolt during surrender ceremonies on Sardinia. The officer in the cockpit was Tenente Colonnello (Lieutenant Colonel) Duilio Fanali the commanding officer of the 51st Stormo. The American officer pointing out items in the cockpit was John C.A. Watkins. (John C. A. Watkins)

Lieutenant Colonel Robert L. Baseler flew this P-51D Mustang, named *Little STUD*, when he was group commander.

Major Herschel H. Green of the 317th FS was an ace with fifteen kills painted on the fuselage under the windscreen.

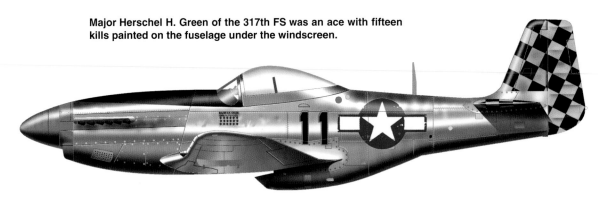

Captain Wayne L. Lowry had the name of his P-51D painted on the starboard side of the aircraft. It was not carried on the port side.

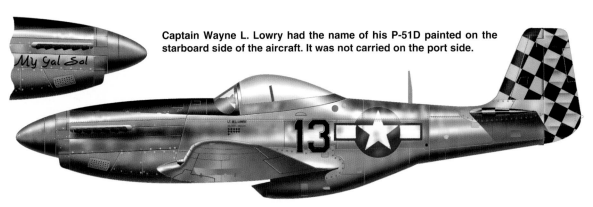

This Mustang, flown by Major Norman L. McDonald of the 318th FS, had two names, a different one on each side of the aircraft.

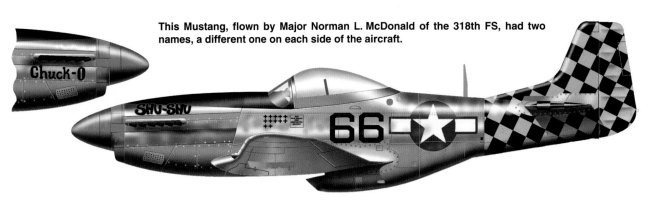

Texas Jessie/Big Mike was flown by Lieutenant William E. Aron of the 318th FS. He was an ace with five kills.

This P-51D was flown by Lieutenant Robert H. Brown of the 318th Fighter Squadron.

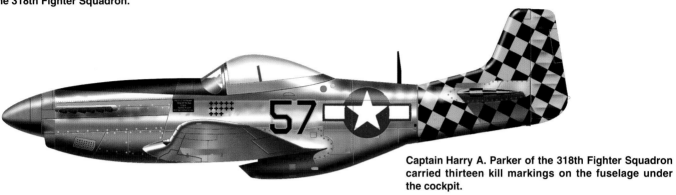

Captain Harry A. Parker of the 318th Fighter Squadron carried thirteen kill markings on the fuselage under the cockpit.

STINKER PAT was a P-51D flown by Major George Hamilton.

THIS IZ IT, was flown by Captain Richard W. Dunkin of the 317 Fighter Squadron. Captain Dunkin carried nine kill markings under the cockpit.

Lieutenant Colonel Chet Sluder flew *SHIMMY IV* on the first shuttle mission to Russia.

Colonel Sluder pins the Distinguished Flying Cross on Lieutenant Hiawatha Mohawk. Mohawk was one of the few Native Americans in the USAAF and was well liked by his crew chief Ed Doss. (Checkertail Clan)

Lieutenant Hiawatha Mohawk straps into the cockpit of his Thunderbolt aided by his crew chief SGT Ed Doss. (Checkertail Clan)

The art work for DALLAS BLONDE came from a Varga girl that appeared in Esquire magazine during 1944. In the original painting the cowgirl had on a Blue outfit with a Yellow tie, White boots, belt, hat and gloves. (Checkertail Clan)

DALLAS BLONDE was flown by Lieutenant Donald Kearns of the 319th Fighter Squadron. The aircraft was named after his first wife. In addition to the nose art, his P-47 had checkered cowling flaps and the standard Red nose ring. (F. Patt)

Herky Green signs off the maintenance check list for his Thunderbolt, indicating that he accepts the aircraft for flight. His crew chief, was Staff SGT "Chuck" Brown. (Checkertail Clan)

Major Lewis B. Chick Jr., commanding officer of the 317th Fighter Squadron, is all smiles as he walks away from HUN HUNTER after completing his last mission. HUN HUNTER, aircraft number 25 was assigned to Lieutenant Eugene H. Emmons, an ace with nine kills all scored in the Thunderbolt. Emmons was assigned to the 318th Fighter Squadron. It was not unusual for squadron commanders to use aircraft assigned to other pilots if their aircraft was not available for a mission. (Bill Chick, Jr.)

(Left) Bob Barkey flew this P-47 named THUNDERBOLT LAD. The aircraft was named for his son. The name was in Yellow and there were three kills under the cockpit. (Bob Barkey)

Major Green also used the Vargas painting on his P-47. This painting was very popular in the Army Air Force and was used on a number of aircraft. (Checkertail Clan)

Captain Hogg looks very pleased after returning from a mission during which he shot down two enemy aircraft with only forty rounds of ammunition. (Roy B. Hogg)

47

Lieutenant John M. Simmons of the 317th Squadron flew this P-51D named *Devastating Dottie*. He was an ace with seven kills.

Bee was an early P-51D flown by Captain Barrie S. Davis.

Captain Barrie S. Davis changed the name on his Mustang to HONEY *Bee* after scoring his first kill. The aircraft carries six German crosses under the cockpit in Black.

MARY MAC carried six kills under the cockpit. She was flown by Lieutenant Gordon H. McDaniel of the 318th FS.

Helen was flown by Captain Auther C. Fiedler of the 317th FS and carried eight kill markings on the fuselage under the windscreen.

This P-51B was named Ski Snoot and was flown by Lieutenant J. R. White. The aircraft crew chief was Jerry Strauss who named the Mustang after his wife. (Jerry Strauss)

to the north, I spotted two contrails and immediately called them out. This time no one said a word, and as they came closer passing about 500 feet above us, it was exhilarating to recognize them as Fw 190s. They looked deadly beautiful. However, nothing happened; no one in our formation went after them. As they turned behind us and disappeared in the haze, I recall an acute feeling of disappointment. This certainly was not the combat I had envisioned. Suddenly on the left side of our formation another airplane materialized flying in the opposite direction. And right behind it were four or five P-51s with several of them firing their guns. Again I could barely contain myself as I recognized the first airplane was an Bf 109 being chopped to pieces from the concentrated machine gun fire of his pursuers.

Of course it was over in an instant as we passed barely 100 yards apart at a closing speed of almost 750 miles per hour, but it was a fantastic experience to be at ringside and see an aircraft literally torn apart on my first mission. This was the kind of combat I had expected.

Returning to base, we landed without incident and were taken to debriefing. I proudly told of the three aircraft I saw and was flabbergasted to hear the "old hands" tell of the forty to fifty enemy aircraft they saw in the area. That was probably the first time I truly understood that there was more to this game of combat than knowing how to fly an airplane. It was my first recognition that one also had to develop an intangible thing called combat sense if he expected to do the job we were there for and survive.

Captain Arthur C. Fiedler, Jr.

Born in Oak Park, Illinois on 1 August 1923. Attended school in Maywood, Illinois graduating from Proviso High in June of 1941. Enlisted in the Cadet program on 28 April 1942, he was put in the enlisted reserve until 26 October 1942 when he was called to active duty and

Colonel Sluder pins the Distinguished Flying Cross on Lieutenant Barrie S. Davis of the 317th Fighter Squadron. (Stan Rosen)

A mixed bag of Mustangs of the 318th Fighter Squadron. Number 47 was flown by Lieutenant Benjamin H. Emmert, Jr., Number 59 was assigned to Lieutenant Fred Wulfe and was named Shu Shu, Number 44, Spirit of Milwaukee County, was flown by Lieutenant Paul Dowd and Number 58A, Charlotte was the mount of Lieutenant Henry E. Southern. (Checkertail Clan)

sent to Nashville, Tennessee for classification. Qualifying for pilot training he was sent to Maxwell Field for preflight and then to Avon Park, Florida for primary, to basic at Macon, Georgia and to advanced at Mariana, Florida. During training he few PT-17s, BT-13s, and AT-6s. After earning his wings and commission he was sent to Richmond, Virginia to fly P-47s, later he became an instructor in the RTU in Dover, Delaware.

He was sent overseas in April of 1944 to join the 325th Group and flew sixty-six combat missions with the Checkertails with 337 hours of combat time. He returned to the States in March of 1945 and was assigned to Craig Field in Selma, Alabama but was not allowed to instruct in the P-40s because he lacked the required time on AT-6s or the Warhawk, which made him a bit bitter!

During his tour with the Clan he was credited with eight victories and one probable, and was the eighth highest scoring Ace with the Group. Art got out of the service after VE day and went to the U. of Illinois but

This P-51C named STROLLING JIM was flown by Lieutenant James O. Granville. The aircraft's name was carried on the starboard side only. (Checkertail Clan)

STROLLING JIM parked on its hardstand in Italy. The P-51D Mustang in the background, number 25, was assigned to Lieutenant Barrie S. Davis. (Cherckertail Clan)

was recalled for the Korean War and was sent to Germany. After Korea he decided to remain in the Air Force. On 1 August 1966 he flew with the 815th TAS operating C-130s and amassed 800 combat hours over some 1,200 sorties. This squadron was the only one to have two Aces assigned to it, the other was Ray Bank. When he retired as a Colonel in 1975 he had been awarded the Silver Star, DFC with Oak Leaf cluster, Air Medal with about twenty-two clusters, the Legion of Merit, the usual theater ribbons plus the Achievement Award as well as a number of Meritorious awards.

Lieutenant Barrie S. Davis

"I'll never forget the day I remained behind to escort some cripples home. We were jumped, but some how only a single 109 remained to press the attack. I latched onto his tail and, unable to shake me, he rolled over and headed straight for the deck. We started the dive at about 25,000 feet and, with everything bent past the firewall we were indicating well past 550 mph passing through 20,000 feet. My guns were spraying the sky, but not a thing was happening to the 109. Finally at about 15,000 feet, bits of his plane began to come off. First a wing tip, then what looked like the cowling and other parts. They streaked past my fuselage, scaring the devil out of me in the process. I couldn't lay a gun on him, although I was shooting from pure fright now. Finally, it must have been below 10,000 feet, the German jettisoned his canopy, struggled upwards, pushed outwards and bailed out. His chute ripped to pieces as he sailed past me. I felt rather sick about

it — *so I guess nobody gets hardened to death."*

"I blacked out when I hauled back on the stick to pull out of the dive. When I came to my plane was flying upward through 18,000 feet and still climbing. Up ahead I saw a burst of flak, and wondered what 20MM flak was doing at 20,000 feet. I broke, right or left, I don't remember, but sitting behind me was another 109! I finally tacked onto his tail and this time my shooting was a bit improved. I knocked out his oil coolers and set him on fire. The oil dumped all over my plane and wrapped up the windshield and wings and I flew blind all the way back to Lesina. The crew chief was upset at all the oil on old Mayfair 24 (radio call sign) because he thought "Honey Bee" was throwing oil out the prop like so many others had come to do. He was most happy to learn it was German oil.

"The most memorable part of the mission? Landing on the perforated steel mat without being able to see any way except out the sides of the canopy."

Barrie finished his tour as a Captain with six victories

Captain Harry Alfred Parker

Captain Harry Alfred Parker was a flight commander and later Operations Officer of the 318th Squadron. He was credited with thirteen victories plus seven damaged and had flown some 273 missions with the 325th before being reported as missing in action. His best day came on 31 July 1944 when he was on a bomber escort mission to Bucharest's Mogosaia Oil Storage Depot The group ran into forty Bf 109s and five Fw 190s at 26,000 feet and as they attacked the Germans

Major Robert M. Barkey of the 319th Fighter Squadron flew this P-51B-15-NA (serial 43-24857), aircraft number 90, that was named Dorothy II after his wife. Other than their checkertails and Red nose bands, the Mustangs were overall Natural Metal with Olive Drab anti-glare panels. (R. M. Barkey)

Major Barkey in the cockpit of *Dorothy II*. The pin-up girl was his personal marking and was carried on the fuselage just forward of the cockpit. The names of his ground crew were, S/SGT A.L. Schneider (crew Chief) and SGT C. Koonce (Assistant Crew Chief). (R. M. Barkey)

went into a huge Lufberry Circle losing altitude all the way down to the deck where the formation broke up. Parker was credited with four Bf 109s destroyed and another six as damaged. This mission made him an Ace with eight kills.

Parker's worst mission came on 12 April 1944, when his P-47 was shot up badly by a P-38 and he was forced to bail out. His first eight kills were scored in a single week and his last came during his second tour, on 14 March 1945. He was lost on a mission to Brux near Vienna on 2 April 1945. He dove to investigate an aircraft flying under his formation and was last seen near Klagenfurth, Austria. Awards earned by Captain Parker included a Silver Star, DFC with cluster, Air Medal with sixteen clusters and the Austrian Partisan Number Two medal presented by the Austrian government.

Captain Parker was born in Pasadena, California on 29 January 1919 and attended school there before his family moved to Merrimac, N.H. He graduated from McGaw Institute in 1933 and spent a year at the University of New Hampshire. He enlisted in the Air Corps in Miami where he was working on 19 October 1940. He was sent to Tampa for basic training then to Chanute Field, Illinois to sheet metal school. He took the test and became an Aviation Cadet and went through training at Maxwell Field, Alabama; Ocala, Florida and Shaw Field in South Carolina. He graduated with pilot wings and was commissioned as a Second Lieutenant at Spence Field, Georgia. He joined the 325th Group in May of 1944. His mother was informed that he was presumed dead on 3 April 1946.

This P-51C Mustang, number 93, was flown by Lieutenant Jack Kinney. The aircraft had the name Mary on the port side of the nose and the name Herman the German on the starboard side.

Benjamin H. Emmert, Jr.

Ben Emmert shot down one enemy aircraft while flying the P-47 and five while flying the P-51. He also was credited with one probable and five damaged. In a strafing mission on the Debrezen Air Field in Hungary on 1 September 1944 he was shot down by flak on his seventh

Captain Phil Crookham (left) and Lieutenant Benjamin H. Emmert, Jr. of the 318th Fighter Squadron. Emmert had one kill while flying P-47s and added five more while flying P-51s. He later added a MiG-15 to his total during the Korean war. (J. W. Cannon)

This Mustang suffered a landing gear failure on landing. A fireman stands by with a hose in case a spark ignites any spilled fuel. The propeller has two undamaged blades, indicating that it was not turning at the time the gear failed. (Checkertail Clan)

The BLONDE SQUAW was the P-51B assigned to Lieutenant Hiawatha Mohawk of the 319th Fighter Squadron. The aircraft carried two victory markings under the cockpit. He scored one on 25 May 1944 and one on 15 June 1944. (Ed Doss)

Lieutenant Paul Dowd crash landed in Milwaukee County. The aircraft came to rest in a field after it struck a ditch off the end of the runway and sheared off the landing gear. The propeller was still turning when the gear ripped away as is evident by the bent blades. (Paul Dowd)

Lieutenant Paul Dowd stands on the wing of his P-51 after he made a crash landing, which ripped off the landing gear. Luckily, the aircraft did not catch fire or strike an immovable object. (Paul Dowd)

The salvage crews are ready to lift Lieutenant Dowd's Mustang and cart it off. The damage to the belly scoop was quite evident and it was doubtful that this Mustang would ever fly again. (Paul Dowd)

pass and captured. He spent the rest of the war as a POW in prison camps in Hungary and Germany. Lieutenant Lowell B. Steel was also shot down by flak on this mission and the group was credited with four air-to-air kills and fifty-nine destroyed on the ground.

Emmert stayed in the Air Force and was a Major when the Korean War broke out in 1950. He was Squadron Operations officer of the 336th Fighter Squadron at Langley AFB. The 4th Fighter Group assumed the air defense role and the 334th went to Newcastle, Delaware, the 335th to Andrews AFB, Maryland and the 336th to Dover, Delaware where they unlocked the gates and reopened the base which had been closed since the end of the Second World War. This was the beginning of the Air Defense Command as it came to be known over the years. The 4th Fighter Group was back in action even if it was only pulling strip alert.

With the advent of the MiG-15s in Korea the Air Force realized that a new fighter was needed to counter the threat. Since the 4th was an F-86A jet fighter outfit with Colonel J. C. Meyer as commander, it got the nod to deploy to Korea. Ben left Dover with a flight of eight less than twelve hours after they were alerted and eventually arrived at Johnson Field, Japan to get ready for posting to Korea. The 336th was the first to go into action with Colonel Bruce Hinton as commander and Emmert as Operations Officer. They operated from Kimpo near Seoul flying several missions before the North Koreans opened their major offensive in December of 1950 that over-ran everything. On 2 January the 336th was forced to evacuate and fall back to Johnson Field. It was February before any part of the outfit went back to Korea, arriving at K-2, which they shared with the 49th Fighter Group. Billy Hovde got in some trouble and Colonel Meyer told Major Emmert to take over the 335th Squadron. He took the 335th to Suwon, Korea where they operated for several months. Late in the Summer of 1951, they moved to Kimpo where they remained until Emmert left for the states in September of 1951. Emmert added another victory in Korea to bring his total to seven, when he downed a MiG-15 and damaged a couple of others. While commander of the 335th, the squadron had fifty-six confirmed kills and did not lose a man. Hoot Gibson (2nd Korean Ace) got four while in Ben's flight. He was leading it the day that Jabara aced out and as Bruce Hinton was scoring his first jet kill Emmert was chasing MiGs off his tail.

Ben Emmert was born 21 March 1920, in Erwin, Tennessee and later attended East Tennessee State University. He graduated from pilot training with class 42-J in November of 1942 at Foster Field, Victoria, Texas and joined the 154th Recon Squadron flying P-39s before transferring to the 325th's 318th Squadron. After Korea he was Commander of the 343rd Fighter Group at Duluth, Minnesota. He retired in January of 1971. He was awarded a Silver Star, DFC w/Cluster, Air Medal with fifteen Oak Leaf Clusters, Purple Heart and the French Criox de Guerre

Lieutenant Dowd's ground crew pose with the ripped off landing gear and the name panel from the port side of the aircraft. Flossie II was Lieutenant Dowd's wife. (Paul Dowd)

Lieutenant Gordon H. McDaniels (left) a native of Sweetwater, Tennessee is congratulated by Captain Harry A Parker of Milford, N.H. after Gordy scored five kills on a single mission. Parker had thirteen kills to his credit before he was shot down while attacking an enemy airfield. (Checkertail Clan)
w/Palm.

Lieutenant Colonel Norman L. McDonald

McDonald was born 21 January 1918 in Framingham, Massachusetts. He graduated from high school and attended Balmont Abbey College in North Carolina. Enrolling in the Civilian Pilot Training program, where he excelled, he went on into the USAAC Cadet program and he won his pilot's wings in December of 1941. He was assigned to the 52nd Fighter Group in May of 1942 in England where he flew Spitfires.

The 2nd Squadron was sent to North Africa and McDonald flew Spitfires during the North African and Sicilian campaigns. He was sent

Bad luck seemed to find the Mustangs flown by Lieutenant Dowd. This aircraft was the one he flew on the first shuttle mission to Russia. Later it was crashed by another pilot.

LADY JEAN, number 72, was flown by Lieutenant John Connelly of the 319th Fighter Squadorn. The aircraft was hit by flak over enemy terretory but was able to make it safely back in spite of the damage to the tail section. (Checkertail Clan)

back to the Zone of the Interior and assigned to a P-47 training squadron at Bradley Field, Connecticut in October of 1943. Soon, tiring of this assignment, he asked for a second combat tour and joined the Checkertails in August of 1944. He was given command of the 318th Squadron and flew a total of 249 missions right up to the war's end in Europe.

He added four victories while with the 325th to bring his total up to eleven and a half along with five probables, seven damaged and a number destroyed on the ground. These feats brought him the DFC w/cluster, the British DFC and the Air Medal w/26 Oak Leaf Clusters.

Captain Wayne L. Lowry

Wayne L. Lowry was a reserve quarterback on the University of Nebraska's football team when he decided to enlist in the National Guard on 5 march 1940. He was called to active duty on 5 March 1941 but it took him a year to transfer to the Army Air Corps and into the Cadet training program. He went through pilot training and was commissioned a Second Lieutenant on 8 October 1942.

Lowry was sent to Tampa, Florida for gunnery training as a fighter pilot and on one mission he got 267 hits on the towed target out of a possible 400, an extremely high total. He was offered a flight instructors rating but passed it up in favor of a combat tour. He was sent to Tallahassee, Florida to be checked out on the P-47. His first instructor told his group of new pilots, "Gentlemen, you start at one end of the runway, gun your engine and by the time you reach the other end we hope you are flying!"

On completion of the training program in the Jug, Lowry was sent to

Ground crewmen remove the ammunition from this damaged P-51B, after the aircraft made a wheels up landing on the PSP runway. (Checkertail Clan)

Hairless Joe was flown by Lieutenant Joe H. Smith of the 319th Fighter Squadron. The aircraft had a hydraulic problem that made it impossible to lock the starboard main landing gear. Luckily for the pilot, the gear did not fail until after the aircraft had slowed. (Checkertail Clan)

join the 325th in North Africa and was assigned to the 317th Squadron. Upon his arrival with his wing man over the Checkertail base he decided to put on a buzz job to let the Group know that they were getting some really hot replacement pilots and proceeded to wring out his bird while still having the belly tank attached much to the chagrin of Colonel Chet Sluder who frowned on such tactics. When they landed Colonel Sluder was waiting to greet them and he did a royal chewing out job on both of them. Captain Lowry was one of the more colorful pilots of the 317th Squadron and was known to be one of the hell bent for leather types

Three Checkertail Aces (left to right) Captain Roy Hogg, Lieutenant Robert M. Barkey and Lieutenant Cullen Hoffman. Hogg had six kills while flying with the 318th FS, two each in the P-40, P-47 and P-51. Hoffman had five, four with the P-47 and one in the P-51. Barkey had five, four with the Thunderbolt and one in the Mustang. (R. M. Barkey)

During his tour Wayne logged about 300 combat hours during sixty-five missions and shot down nine Bf 109s and two Fw 190s plus destroying six enemy transports on the ground during strafing missions. Wayne shot down his first six enemy aircraft in a period between 6 June 1944 and 24 June 1944. His seventh kill earned him the Silver Star. Wayne downed four more enemy planes before he ran out of gas on a mission and had to bail out over occupied territory. He landed successfully and hid his chute under a fodder stack. The shock when his chute had opened caused him to lose his .45, his wallet and as usual he had forgotten his dog tags. When he was captured after walking three miles he had nothing to prove that he actually was a pilot and although he was walked back the three miles he couldn't find his chute so his status was still in doubt. He finally was able to convince his captors that he was a pilot and after a number of days had passed he finally was sent to Stalag Luft I near Barth on the Baltic Sea. On the train he met all kinds of Kreigesgefangeners, the German term for POWs including a Piper Cub pilot who had been shot down while spotting for the artillery, glider pilots and even paratroopers. They arrived at the POW camp on 1 November 1944. At that time the ranking Allied officer was Colonel

Penrod was flown by Captain Roy B. Hogg. The aircraft was later transferred to the 4th Fighter Group in England to replace Major Howard "Deacon" Hiverly's Mustang which had been badly shot up on a mission to Budapest on 2 July 1944. It ended up being bellied in on 17 November 1944 and was written off.

Lieutenant Eugene H. Emmons in the cockpit of his P-51B Mustang with nine kills on the fuselage under the cockpit. He did not use any name on his Mustang, probably because he had been ordered to remove the Hun Hunter name from his Thunderbolt by higher authority. (Ira Grandel)

Roy Hogg was very fond of dogs and would pass out cigars when his female dog presented him with a litter of puppies. A pair of these pups are with him here. (Roy. B. Hogg)

Henry Spicer who had been the CO of the 355th Group's 357th Squadron. Since Wayne spoke some German he got along fairly well in the camp as he was able to swap items in his Red Cross parcels with the guards for things he lacked. By the time the war had reached the stage where the guards simply deserted, Colonel Francis Gabreski was the ranking officer in camp. He detailed some of the men to take over the guard towers to keep the POWs from taking off on their own but soon the Russians arrived and a tank ran over the front gate saying" let the men go, they've been POWs for a long time." Many, including Wayne, took off and walked about 20 miles a day. Finally he asked a Russian officer for food was given a loaf of bread and stuck in a displaced persons camp. He escaped the same night and kept walking until he came on to the American lines and was home at last. For him the war was over.

After returning home he remained in the Reserve and in February of 1957 he was called to active duty as a Lieutenant Colonel and served with the 439th FBW at Selfridge Field, Michigan until I May 1957. During this time he successfully completed the jet Qualification Course at Craig AFB, Alabama. He retired as a Colonel in August of 1957 and

Delightful Dee was a P-51B (serial 43-024852) flown by Lieutenant Arthur Albin of the 319th Fighter Squadron. The aircraft was lost on 12 October 1944 while being flown by Lieutenant Videto on a strafing mission in the Budapest area. (H. L. Cramer)

SOCKO, a P-51C, number 78, of the 319th Fighter Squadron crashed and burned. The crash crews have opened the ammunition bays to make sure that all unexploded ammunition has been removed from the wreck. (Checkertail Clan)

held a co-pilots job with Zantrop Air Lines

Captain Robert M. Barkey

Bob Barkey, a native of Michigan, graduated from Wyandotte High School and then attended Michigan State University before joining the Wyandotte Police Force as an officer. He later enlisted in the Army Air Forces Aviation Cadet program and was called to active duty on 9 October 1942. After winning his pilots wings at Brooks Field, Texas he eventually was sent to Casablanca on 4 October 1943 arriving there on 18 October. He was then sent to the 325th Fighter Group's 319th Squadron.

During his tour with the Checkertails Captain Barkey flew fifty-three combat missions in both the P-47 and P-51 logging 200 hours and 10 minutes of combat flying earning the DFC, Air Medal, with 12 Oak Leaf clusters, three battle stars and a Presidential Unit Citation. Barkey shot down five Bf 109s and was credited with a probable on a Macchi 202. Bob became a flight leader during his tour, flew forty-five missions in

Stormy Gail was assigned to the 318th Fighter Squadron and carried the aircraft number 59. The Mustang was flown by Lieutenant William H. Walker.

This unidentified P-51 on fire in the middle of the field seems to have made a power-on belly landing as indicated by the bent propeller blades. (Checkertail Clan)

his P-47 "Thunderbolt Lad" named after his young son and eight missions in his P-51B "Dorothy II" named after his wife.

Scoring his first victory on 22 January 1944, Bob recalled, "When we first saw the enemy planes, they were flying a line abreast string formation. I pulled in on the tail of one of the Bf 109s and was within thirty yards when I got in a good burst at his belly and tail. I could see pieces coming off his plane as he did a half roll and crashed."

Upon completion of his tour he was rotated back to the States and sent

Lieutenant William H. Walker (left) was the pilot of Stormy Gail. He was assigned to the 318th Fighter Squadron and flew on the first shuttle mission to Russia. (Checkertail Clan)

to Hillsgrove, R. I., to become an instructor. While there during the Sixth War Loan drive Bob was credited with selling over $8,000,000 worth of War Bonds by means of public appearances.

Ground Crews

Every pilot knew how valuable the men in his ground crew were since his life depended upon them. The long hours, under difficult conditions, they put in to keep him flying were fully appreciated.

In North Africa tools often had to be kept in a pail of aviation gasoline to keep them cool enough to use since even a few minutes laying in the desert sun made them too hot to handle. In addition, tools themselves were hard to come by and spare parts were in such short supply that any time a plane made a crash landing mechanics would rush out to salvage parts.

Living conditions, especially in North Africa, were very primitive and unlike the officers, the enlisted men were stuck for the duration of the war since there was no rotation plan for them. So they were overseas for the entire war.

Brigadier General Ralph G. Taylor, Jr. recalled that he flew seven different aircraft, all named the Duchess of Durham during his tour. One of them set a record of over 100 hours without a spark plug change.

ANNABELL flipped over on its back, crushing the fin and rudder and bending the propeller shaft. The cause of the accident may have been a dip in the ground that caused the nose to dip and the propeller to strike the ground. (Checkertail Clan)

BOSS BABY, number 86, was another Mustang that suffered a hydraulic failure and suffered damage as a result of a failed main landing gear leg. The aircraft was flown by Lieutenant Harry S. Carroll of the 319th Fighter Squadron. (Checkertail Clan)

Herky Green flew this P-51C Mustang, number 11. At this time he had fourteen kills, although he soon added another to become a triple Ace.

Major Green and his crew chief, SGT Stranski next to his P-51C (serial 42-103324). This aircraft suffered category two flak damage on 21 November 1944 and was salvaged for parts. (Checkertail Clan)

Linda Joyce and Belligerent Betts share the PSP ramp at the group's home base at Rimini, Italy. Belligerent Betts was flown by Lieutenant Colonel Ernie Beverly and Linda Joyce was flown by Lieutenant Jerry Heimbach. Colonel Beverly's Mustang was named by his crew chief, Technical Sergeant Larry Lang, who named it in honor of his girl friend. (H. L. Cramer)

"Jack Evens was my crew chief and the person responsible for that achievement. Evans crewed old number 13 through the war." Evans recalled that the box score of number 13 during the war was twenty-six confirmed victories and about 250 missions. Zack Taylor became the first MTO Ace flying number 13. "Herky" Green flew it just once and scored his first victory but got so badly shot up he switched to number 11. Wayne Lowry had eleven victories in number 13 before becoming MIA. At the time Evans was on a three day pass and wondered and worried about why Wayne was lost until they met at a reunion after the war and Wayne told him that he had simply run out of gas. Others who flew number 13 included Warren Sibley who changed the name to "Whiz Kid", Neil Carroll, Bass, Forte, Brewer and Dan Penrod. Number 13 was the first P-47 to fly in North Africa.

Evans and Ira Grandell were the two crew chiefs who were selected to accompany the group to Russia on Operation FRANTIC JOE, by riding in one of the B-17s. On the way back the one Evens was in took fifty-seven bullet holes.

Colonel Chet Sluder's crew chief was Luke Meisenheimer and Chet was very appreciative of the long hours he put in working to keep "Shimmy" in top condition and wished *That I could have gotten a few more victories for Luke's sake.*

Ed Doss was Hiawatha Mohawk's crew chief and he was so highly regarded by Mohawk that whenever Hiawatha managed to get some

The individual aircraft number (77) on Belligerent Betts was outlined in Yellow as was the pilot and crew name plates (Yellow was the squadron color for the 319th FS). This was the last style of checker application on the Mustang, with the checkertail extending up forward of the fin extension. (E. H. Beverly)

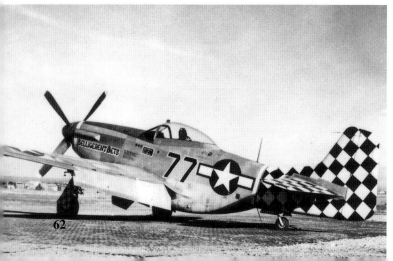

Colonel Beverly climbs into his P-51C on 17 July 1944, the day after he scored his first kill, which was quickly added to the side of his Mustang. (E. H. Beverly)

Lieutenant Colonels Fexil L. Vidal and Ernie Beverly at the opening of the 325th new officers club on 1 November 1944. Captain Don Lynch talked a AAA battery into setting up search lights to provide a Hollywood type grand opening night. General Twining attended the opening. All the work needed to turn the old stable into a club was done by the men themselves.

General Nate Twining congratulates Lieutenant Colonel Beverly after awarding him the Distinguished Flying Cross. (Checkertail Clan)

Belligerent Betts and Hells Outcast (78) provide a backdrop for the 319th FS' memorial tribute to President Roosevelt on receiving the news of his death. Hells Outcast was flown by Lieutenant Paul C. Dickens. (Checkertail Clan)

THISIZIT with two unidentified ground crewmen. The regular crew for the Mustang was S/SGT W. Bush (Crew Chief), SGT J. Blackburn (Assistant Crew Chief), J. Leach and C. Riely (Armorers) and G. Hendricks (Radio Technician). (Stan Wilson)

good booze he shared it with Ed.

Bob Baseler's crew chief, Clem Eckert, took a good natured ribbing from Bob because he had a laugh that sounded like Mortimer Snerd, one of Edgar Bergen's ventriloquist dummys. Clem finally told Bob that if he didn't quit calling him Mortimer Snerd he was going to paint that name on his P-40. Baseler told him that he wouldn't dare, but next morning Bob found the name in bright red and yellow letters on the nose of his P-40.

Major Richard M. Dunkin flew THISIZIT, a P-51D-5-NA (serial 44-13336), number 7 of the 317th Fighter Squadron. Major Dunkin was an Ace with nine kills painted on the side of the fuselage under the cockpit.

Lieutenant George Novotny (second from right) and his ground crew, S/SGT R. E. Ebert (Crew Chief), SGT E. F. McGregory (Armorer), SGT F. P. Newman (Radio) and an unidentified member of the crew, in front of his Mustang, number 27. (Checkertail Clan)

Another crew chief, Gerald Strauss , was of German descent and could read the language. He was often called on to translate various instrument panel warnings on captured Luftwaffe aircraft.

Crew chiefs did all of the mechanical work including engine, propeller, brake, and hydraulic repairs. Each chief had an assistant, equally qualified, plus a radio man and an armorer in his crew. Each man took pride in doing his job well. These men were typical of the crew men who helped make the 325th one of the finest groups of the Second World War.

Lieutenant Philip Sangermano

Philip Sangermano was a native of Peterborough, New Hampshire and was one of five aces from the state of New Hampshire. He was one of ten children and had graduated from Peterbourough High School in 1942 just in time to enlist in the USAAF Cadet program. He entered Cadet training on 9 February 1943, was sent to Maxwell Field, Alabama for Preflight training, to Primary at Camden, Arkansas, and received his wings on 3 November 1943 at Craig Field, Alabama.

He was 20 years old when he was listed as MIA on 9 December and had flown fifty-nine missions. He was credited with eight enemy aircraft in air-to-air combat and had five more as destroyed on the ground. For these actions he was awarded the DFC, Air Medal and the Bronze Star.

It was learned later that he had been injured when he was shot down and made a crash landing in Italy. Italian farmers pulled him from the wreckage of "Maty Norris", his P-51C (aircraft number 61). They hid him from the Germans for two weeks but they were unable to bring in a doctor to treat his wounds. He died of his injuries and they buried him. After the war, his family had his body exhumed and returned home for a

Major James V. Toner's Mustang was coded 00. This P-51D Mustang also had the wingtips and landing gear doors checked. Major Toner was the commander of the 318th FS and as CO he had the option of selecting a double digit aircraft number. He was credited with three kills. (Checkertail Clan)

Lieutenant George P. Novotny of Toledo, Ohio was awarded the Distingished Flying Cross and the Air Medal with thirteen Oak Leaf Clusters. He was an Ace with eight kills and flew over fifty combat missions. (Checkertail Clan)

final burial.

Lieutenant George P. Novotny

George Novotny was born in Toledo, Ohio on 22 February 1920. He went to Waite High School, and then to DeSales College in his home town where he excelled in football. His football jersey carried a big 27 on the back and upon joining the 325th he was assigned to aircraft number 27. His crew chief was Staff Sergeant R. E. Ebert who named all of his aircraft "LADY JANE." Novotny flew "LADY JANE VI" with the name "RUTHLESS RUTHIE" on the left side of the nose. George also flew a P-40 numbered 27.

His combat record was eight victories and two enemy aircraft damaged and this record earned him the DFC and the Air Medal with fourteen OLCs plus two Presidential Unit Citations. When he completed his combat tour he was returned to the States and served as an instructor for French pilot trainees. When the war ended he took his discharge and went back to college to finish his education.

Lieutenant Gordon H. McDaniel

A native of Sweetwater Tennessee, McDaniel scored his six kills on just two missions and was one of a number of Aces who got five victories on a single mission. His first victory was scored on the Group's 400th mission, a fighter sweep.

On 14 March 1945, the Clan took off from Rimini at 1020 to provide penetration, target and withdrawal support for the B-24s of the 55th Bomb Wing that were raiding the Novo Zamky marshalling yards in Hungary. On the return flight McDaniels found himself unable to believe his own eyes, as strung out in single file below him was a flight of eight or nine Fw 190s, a perfect formation for his attack. He slid onto the tail of the last one and shot it down, moved on to the next in line and shot him down. He nailed the next three with ease and even got to within 100 feet of one before he was noticed, but by then it was too late. The others finally spotted him and fled. All six of Gordons kills were Fw 190s.

McDaniel flew aircraft number 40 , named "Mary Mac" a P-51D-10-

A flight of 15th Air Force fighters over the Alps during a figher group commander's meeting. Number 00 was flown by Major James V. "Buzz" Toner, deputy commander of the 325th. Number 7 was flown by Colonel Benjamin O. Davis, commander of the 332nd Fighter Group. WD-Q was assigned to Colonel Marion Malcom of the 52nd FG. The last Mustang, HL-A, was the mount of Colonel William A. Daniel of the 31st Group. Colonel Benjamin O. Davis would later become the first Black General Officer in the Air Force. (via Jeff Ethell)

Major Max McNeil was commander of the 317th Fighter Squadron from 23 September 1944 to 3 April 1945. He replaced Major Herky Green when Green completed his tour and was rotated back to the United States. (Stanley Rosen)

This P-51D Mustang (serial 44-14452), aircraft 32 of the 317th Fighter Squadron was flown by Major Max McNeil, the squadron commander. The Mustang carried the name *Marlice Jo* under the exhaust stacks. (via Jeff Ethell)

Colonel Ben Davis, commander ot the 332nd Fighter Wing, in Mustang number 7, is flanked by the deputy commander of the 325th (number 00, Major Toner). On either end of the flight are the commanders of the 309th Fighter Squadron (WZ-B) and 4th Fighter Squadron (WD-X) of the 52nd Fighter Group. The occasion of this unusual formation was a fighter group commander's meeting. (via Jeff Ethell)

NA (44-14467) formerly flown by Jim Toner. This plane later was lost in action while being flown by Paul J. Murphy who cut in front of Norm McDonald who was chasing a Bf 109.

Nothing Fazes A Good Man

Shortly after arriving in Italy, the 325th Fighter Group was struck by a violent storm with extremely high winds. The storm caused a lot of damage and many tents collapsed. Of course everyone was scurrying around, checking the downed tents to be sure no one inside had been injured. Several men ran to the fallen tent of an unnamed squadron commander and cursed the luck when they found him lying on his cot. They quickly found, however, that he had a companion — a bottle of Irish Whiskey that had been liberated from the British forces in the area. No record exists of the conversation that occurred but, according to unusually reliable sources, this unnamed squadron commander made it abundantly clear that his would-be rescuers were to GET OUT and LEAVE HIM ALONE. Rumors state that he and his companion were still in the cot even after the tent was re-erected. Just another

example of the hardships we had to face.

Even Aces Boo Boo

Our Group's pilots on many occasions cursed P-38 Groups as they, not infrequently, made a hasty ID and mistook our P-40s and P-51s for a Bf 109 with varying consequences. However, it may be that P-38s were not the only culprits, perhaps some of us also failed the air-

Jack Evans and Wayne Lowry discuss a point regarding the drop tanks on Lowry's P-51.

Lieutenant Wayne Lowry flew a Mustang with the individual aircraft number 13. He scored a total of eleven kills before he was forced to bail out on a mission and became a POW. (Wayne Lowry)

A line-up of P-51Ds of the 317th Fighter Squadron. Number 22, *Rosemary F* was flown by Lieutenant George Wynmore, Number 10, *STINKER PAT*, was flown by Lieutenant George Hamilton and was named after his infant son. The eyes painted on the aircraft behind the exhaust stacks were looking back to keep his tail clear. (via Dan Penrod)

craft identification process.

In an unnamed squadron, on an unspecified mission, our P-51s were in the process of mixing it up with a gaggle of Bf 109s which were trying to hit the deck and scatter. As this melee surged toward the ground, one of the P-51s opened fire on a Bf 109 that he had closed on — an apparent '109 that is, because immediately the wingman's radio blared with, "(Unnamed Name), that's a 51 your on!" The 109/51 was fortunate and escaped death from the bullets of one of our aces. After landing and reaching his revetment, the ace was observed opening his gun camera and insuring the film was fully developed by the sunlight. During the after-mission briefing, one of the other squadron pilots told about being blasted by a 109 that he had never seen!! The usual platitudes were offered about looking around, keeping your head out of your buttock and that apparently was the end of it.

About a week later at one of the pre-mission briefings, it was announced that in repairing the shot-up P-51, it was discovered that several bullets were still in his fuselage tank and upon recovering them, it was learned that they were not German bullets, but good old American .50 caliber slugs. As the Commander emphasized the importance of identifying your target before firing, one certain individual was observed slouching so far down in his seat, that we were afraid he was going disappear down a knothole in the floor.

A flight of Mustangs from the 318th Fighter Squadron over Italy. Number 40 was flown by Lieutenant Colonel James V. Toner, Jr. Number 43, Stonewall II, was the mount of Lieutenant Leroy B. Raymond. Raymonds aircraft had the short version of the checkertail markings, while the commander's aircraft had the full style. (Checkertail Clan)

Lieutenant Colonel James V. Toner, Jr. of West Roxbury, Mass was awarded the Silver Star for his action on 6 June 1944, when his flight attacked a superior force of about thirty enemy aircraft. His flight was successful in driving off the enemy from their attack on a bomber group. During this action he was also credited with saving the life of a fellow pilot by driving off two enemy fighters that were attacking him. He had three confirmed victories during his tour as commander of the 318th Fighter Squadron. (Checkertail Clan)

General Taylor visited the 325th at the time when Lieutenant Colonel Waytt P. Exum (center) replaced Colonel Vidal as commander of the 325th (6 June 1945). Exum had previously served a tour in the Pacific with the 49th Fighter Group. The three pilots each have different wings. General Taylor has Command Pilot wings, Colonel Exum has Senior Pilot wings and Major "Doc" Watkins has standard pilot wings. Command and Senior pilot wings are awarded based on the number of flight hours a pilot has accumulated.

It's A Small World — Les Long

We were returning from a mission when we picked up a distress call on the radio from a B-17 that was in trouble over Yugoslavia. Alone, with one engine out, he obviously was very scared.

My flight leader located him and our flight of four started to escort him home. It soon became apparent that the pilot of the B-17 was absolutely terrified and would not let us out of his sight. Two of us had to fly his wing - one on each side, while the other two P-51s could climb above him for proper protection.

Unfortunately, in a few minutes, another engine quit and the crew jettisoned anything and everything that was not bolted down. But it was in vain as almost immediately the third engine quit and the crew announced that they would have to bail out.

We circled around watching them bail out like paratroopers and followed the B-17 which made a few swings left and right before crash-

Lieutenant Dan Penrod of the 317th Fighter Squadron flew some twenty-nine combat missions with the 325th. He is now the head of the Checkertail reunion committee and edits the "Roll Call" the association news bulletin. (Dan Penrod)

ing into the side of a mountain. We kept an eye on the crew and followed their progress as they landed in, on, and around a farmers house. One landed on a red tile roof, one in a tree beside the house and the others were very close. There was nothing more we could do so waggling our wings, we took off for home.

Several weeks later, four or five of us were sent on R&R to the Isle

MOLLY, a P-51D of A Flight, 319th Fighter Squadron on the ramp at Foggia Main, Italy in May of 1945. The Mustang was flown by Lieutenant "Cotton" Addis. His crew chief was Art Comny. (via Larry Davis)

of Capri. While having lunch on the patio of the Quissisanna Hotel, several Air Force men joined us at our table.

You know the conversation: "What do you fly?" "B-17's" "How many missions?" "ONE!" "What are you doing at rest camp?" we asked. "We went down in Yugoslavia on our first mission," was the reply. "Glad you made it, but which one were you? Did you land on the red tile roof or in the tree?" I asked. "No, I landed on the red tile roof ... but wait a minute, how do you know where we landed?" came the surprised answer. "Remember the black and yellow Checkertail P-51s who escorted you down?" I replied.

From then on it was happy time — and we had a long, pleasant conversation. There is nothing fantastic about this story except what were the odds of us ever meeting the crew of that B-17?

A Helping Hand Can Get You Into Trouble — Dan Penrod

Returning from a mission over Germany, Robert (Bob) Findley Gayle and I spotted a lone B-24 with one engine feathered lumbering along well below us. Contacting him on the radio, I learned he had one engine out, another that was very sick and obviously was elated when I confirmed that we would escort him. We dropped down beside him and a few moments later they began to jettison everything that wasn't nailed down in an attempt to maintain altitude. Guns, ammunition, boxes, miscellaneous equipment, and many unknown objects streamed out of their waist positions for what seemed like minutes. All that was missing was the proverbial kitchen sink.

Although it would have made a better story, the Luftwaffe did not intercept us, and we escorted the bomber back to Italy. They had obviously noted our numbers and markings as that night I received a call from the pilot who told me he had been decorated for bringing his bird back and wanted Bob and I to come to their base so they could show their appreciation.

As it happened there was no mission the next day and not wanting to

Lieutenant Robert H. Brown started out as a Flight Officer with the 318th Fighter Squadron. He became an Ace with a total of seven kills. Three of these came on a single mission on 28 June 1944, when he shot down three Bf 109s. All of his kills came within a two month period. (Checkertail CLan)

Lieutenant Geroge Hamilton's STINKER PAT had eyes that watched his tail. Hamilton named his aircraft after his young son. The aircraft's smile and blood shot eyes were the same Red as the nose band. (Stan Wilson)

Number 42 made a crash landing and had the main landing gear fail. It was just one of many to suffer this type of accident. (Checkertail Clan)

(Above & Below) Major John R. Burman flew this P-51D named THREE BEES. The aircraft had three small cartoon bees on the fuselage behind the name and a larger bee under the name, Major Burman even had his drop tanks painted in checks. (Checkertail Clan)

miss some free drinks, we borrowed a jeep and late in the afternoon drove down to the bomber base. What a surprise! They were delighted to meet us, and escorted us their club where we were received like heroes. They toasted our bravery, daring, and just about anything else they could think of. These accolades continued with round after round of drinks as we became increasingly embarrassed for what we knew to be an every day occurrence. Each time I tried to explain that any fighter pilot would have done the same thing, they just laughed, toasted our modesty, and kept telling us how great we were. The more we protested, the worse it got.

Finally it reached the point that even though three sheets to the wind, I became so embarrassed that I could take no more of it. Winking at Bob, I announced in a loud voice that the real reason we had escorted their bird was not that we were concerned about them, but had hoped that it would serve as bait, bring out some German fighters and give us a chance to get in some action. From the abrupt silence that ensued, I realized I had committed the ultimate faux pas, but before I could explain, as the saying goes, the fat was in the fire.

Immediately, the mood turned ugly and our buddies of a few minutes ago turned on Bob and me with a vengeance. Harsh words and names poured out, a few blows were thrown, and for a little while I was concerned for our safety. However, cooler heads prevailed and calm was restored. I tried to apologize explaining that what I said was in jest because we were really tremendously embarrassed by all their praise. They appeared to grudgingly accept my explanation; however, the magic that existed shortly before was irretrievably lost and the party rapidly wound down.

Hells Bells was the 325th two seat Mustang. It was used for VIP flights and to indoctrinate new pilots. It also served to give ground crews a feel of what it was like to fly in the aircraft they worked on. The aircraft had partially checked drop tanks and checked landing gear doors. (Checkertail Clan)

Helene and Baby too, was the P-51D Mustang assigned to Lt Gerald B. Edwards of the 317th Fighter Squadron. The aircraft carried the side number 38. Edwards was credited with three kills. (Checkertail Clan)

Number 18 was named STOUT BURR BON and was flown by Lieutenant Robert S. Bass. The name was painted on the cowling under the exhaust stacks in such a way as to make it look out of focus, like the viewer had one too many shots of "Burrbon". (Stan Wilson)

Co-Pilot On A P-51! — Les Long

Some stories of the 325th are the result of bravery, some occurred by accident, and some by good planning. As I think about this story, it probably should be classified as stupidity but back then — who cared.

The date was 26 August 1944, and we were on a mission to Otopen A/D. For some reason, my right wing began to leak gas and after a couple of hours, it became evident that if I continued to the target, I would not get back to our base.

So Harold Loftus, Vernon Bradeen, and I headed back to Spinazolla to refuel. But my troubles were not over as when I landed, I found I had a flat tire. The bomb group did not have a P-51 tire, our B-25 was out of operation for repairs, and the prospect of spending several days on a bomber base did not appeal to me.

After talking it over, Harold decided the two of us would fly to

Major Ralph Johnson was commander of the 319th Fighter Squadron from 7 December 1944 until May of 1945. On 18 April 1945 he shot down a Me-262 jet fighter. (Stan Rosen)

STOUT BURR BON in flight over the Alps. While the mountains were very beautiful, they were very dangerous. In the event of an engine failure in the single engine Mustang, the pilot had little chance. (Checkertail Clan)

71

"Dusty Butt" was the personal aircraft of one of the 325th commanders, Colonel Felix Vidal. The aircraft had formerly been named Belligerent Betts when it was flown by Colonel Beverly, who turned it over to Felix "Pic" Vidal. Colonel Vidal later crashed the aircraft. (Stan Wilson)

Lesina in his P-51. Operations cleared us with Loftus listed as pilot, Long as co-pilot. Bradeen told them he was not taking a co-pilot on this flight. I wore my chute, without the life raft or cushion and Loftus sat on my lap without a chute. As the song goes, "Off we go ... or went!"

I tried to convince Loftus that we should drop the wing tanks to make for an easier landing, but his theory was that if we wrecked the plane during the landing, he could blame it on the tanks.

Landing at Lesina was interesting. Harold flew our normal 1/4 loop pattern and if you weigh 120 pounds and had a 150 pounder on your lap, you can imagine how heavy he became in that pitch out. My sole contribution to the landing was to operate the wheels and flaps as Harold could not reach them. But no problem, he made a beautiful landing.

We were quite pleased as we had made it home safe and sound. All was well until Headquarters called the Squadron informing them that: "All your pilots are back, but one plane is listed as missing. Find out what happened and see that it does not happen again!" Phase Two had just begun.

Very soon word came for Long and Loftus to report to the Executive Officer. We both decided that obviously we are up for a court-martial so we might as well try to talk our way out of it.

Major Ralph F. Johnson in Colonel Vidal's "Dusty Butt" over the east coast of Italy. Johnson was commander of the 319th Fighter Squadron. (Checkertail Clan)

Since it was my plane that was missing, the Exec started on me and after I explained our problems to him, he clarified to us — in a military fashion, his viewpoint!! Why would I put my life in Loftus' hands? I pointed out that I had flown on Harold's wing for six to eight missions, and I considered him the best pilot in the squadron. "But what if you had to bail out?" he persisted. "No problem," I replied, "I was wearing the only parachute." "But Loftus was on your lap. You didn't expect him to bail out with no chute?"

With a nothing ventured, nothing gained attitude, I pulled out my G.I. issue knife, flipped it on the desk and told the Exec that Harold and I had discussed this very same problem. I told Harold that if we had to bail out he might as well jump because if he didn't, I was going to stick this knife right between his shoulder blades. He was in a no-win situation (this might explain why Harold never flew above 100 feet all the way home.)

When the Exec stopped laughing, he told us to get out of his office but to walk the ramp as punishment. We did about a week later and never heard any more about the incident.

Harold put it this way, "There are many things we would have done differently had we the experience to know the difference at the time, but we did the best we could and survived", and that about says it all.

Although our ride was downright foolish, it should not be forgotten that Major Exum and a number of others landed in enemy territory and using this same procedure, rescued downed pilots who otherwise would have been POWs. It should also be noted that a number of pilots failed in these attempts and eventually orders were issued that any further attempts at this type of rescue would result in a court-mar-

Colonel Vidal congratulates SGT Rowland W. Woodword of Chicago, IL for his outstanding performance as crew chief on "Dusty Butt". The other officer is believed to be Major Sherman Hoar, the group maintenance officer. (Earl Rienhart)

Sissy Squirt, aircraft number 38, was flown by Lieutenant Gerald B. Edwards. Edwards was credited with three kills. (Checkertail Clan)

Hell's Angel was the Mustang flown by Lieutenant Ralph L. Fort of Pekin, Il. Number 11 had been assigned to Herky Green during his tour and his eighteen victories made him the top scorer in the group and second within the theater. (R. L. Fort)

tial even if successful. Officialdom decided that the possibility of losing two aircraft instead of one did not justify the risk.

Hairless Joe, was flown by Lieutenant Joe H. Smith. It was the second Mustang to carry this name, the first was an early P-51B. (Stan Wilson)

Major Norman McDonald was commander of the 318th Fighter Squadron from 26 Novermber 1944 until May of 1945. He came to the group from the 52nd Fighter Group. While with the 52nd he scored seven kills and added another four while with the 325th for a total of eleven. (Stanley Rosen)

SHU-SHU was the Mustang assigned to Major Norman McDonald commander of the 318th Fighter Squadron. Major McDonald did not carry kill markings on his Mustang, even though he had seven kills while with the 52nd Fighter Group and four more while with the 325th. He was the last commander of the 318th FS. (via Jeff Ethell)

SQUEEZIE was a P-51D that carried a number of different names during its career. Number 79 was flown by several pilots, each of which changed the aircraft's name. At this time the Mustang was being flown by Lieutenant Stanley DeGeer. (Stan Wilson)

Number 79 was also flown by Captain George R. Bland. Ed Doss was his crew chief and the Mustang was now named Janie Baby. (Ed Doss)

BALLZOUT II was a P-51D (serial 44-13440) flown by Lieutenant Walter R. "Billy" Hinton. Hinton was an Ace with a total of five kills. (Stan Wilson)

(Right) BALLZOUT II had the artwork applied before the name. Hinton used the "Spitin Kitten" tiger as his personal marking. This was the second Mustang to carry the name, the first was a P-51C that he flew on the first shuttle mission to Russia. (Stan Wilson)

Lieutenant Cullen J. Hoffman flew number 39 while with the 317th Fighter Squadron. After he finished his tour, the P-51D was transferred to the 319th Squadron, renumbered as 94 and assigned to Lieutenant D. E. Ambrose. (Checkertail Clan)

Lieutenant Hoffman's number 39 did not carry a name. Hoffman was an Ace with five kills. His crew chief was S/SGT Charles Brown (left) who had been Herky Green's crew chief. CPL Buford Paisley (right) was Brown's assistant. (via Jeff Ethell)

A flight of P-51Ds of the 317th Fighter Squadron, 325th Fighter Group. Number 30 was BALLZOUT II, the mount of Lieutenant Walter R. Hinton. (Larry Davis)

(Right) Number 39 was later reassigned to Lieutenant David E. Ambrose who renamed it Miss Cathie. He had two kills painted on the fuselage. His second kill was scored on 19 January 1945. (James V. Crow)

(Lower Right) HONEY JO was a P-51D (serial 44-15378) flown by Lieutenant Sheldon K. Anderson. Anderson shot down two Bf 109s and a Fw 190 on 16 October 1944 along with two probables and a damaged. The mission was a raid on the oil refinery at Brux, Czechoslovakia. He was shot down on 13 March 1945 and became a POW. After the war an airport in Wisconsin was named in his honor. (David W. Weatherill)

The tail markings of the B-24 in the background identify it as belonging to the 485th Bomb Group. The White Liberator is a PB4Y-1 of the Navy. The 485th was one of the bomb groups that was escorted on a regular basis by the 325th. (James V. Crow)

A flight of P-51D Mustangs of the 317th Fighter Squadron take the runway for another mission. Aircraft number 31 was flown by Lieutenant Edsel Paulk, an Ace with five kills (all scored in P-47s) and number 25 was flown by Lieutenant Eugene H. Emmons who also scored all of his nine kills flying the Thunderbolt. (Stan Wilson)

This Mustang was named "BUCKO" and was flown by Lieutenant Roy Carbee. The aircraft carries the short version of the tail checkers. (Stan Wilson)

"Doris D" was another rename of aircraft number 79 although the pilot was unknown. It was not uncommon for aircraft to undergo a number of name changes as pilots completed their tours and the Mustangs were assigned to other pilots. (Stan Wilson)

This P-51D was named MARY NELL and was flown by Lieutenant William A. Taylor of the 317th Fighter Squadron. (Checkertail Clan)

The Third Dallas Blonde was the name of this Mustang flown by Donald Kearns of the 319th Fighter Squadron. (Checkertail Clan)

(Left) Ginny B of the 317th Fighter Squadron takes off on another mission. The aircraft, a P-51D (serial 42-103517) was flown by Lieutenant Arne E. Aho (Checkertail Clan)

RED, was a P-51D Mustang flown by Lucien Phillips for his tour. Later, the Mustang was reassigned to Lieutenant A. L. Christo. The name was carried on both sides of the cowling. (Stan Wilson)

JAN'S LITTLE JOE was aircraft number 63. The P-51D Mustang was flown by Lieutenant Joel Mason. His personal insignia, a pair of dice, reflected a "little Joe," or a pair of deuces. (J. W. Cannon)

(Below) SGT Jack Evans was crew chief on My Gal Sal, which he named after his wife. He crewed number 13 throughout the war and never had an abort due to mechanical problems. On one mission, Lieutenant Wayne Lowry hit a tree on a strafing run and Jack pulled a fifteen inch branch out of the Mustang's carburetor air intake. (Jack Evans)

Devastating Dottie, aircraft number 27 of the 317th Fighter Squadron, carried the name Lady Janie VIII on the starboard side of the nose. The aircraft was flown by Captain John M. Simmons an Ace with seven kills. Simmons was later killed in a T-33 crash at Eglin AFB.

Ground crews work on the engine of Stormy Gail, the P-51D Mustang flown by Lieutenant William H. Walker of the 318th Fighter Squadron. The Mustang carried the side number 59. (via Larry Davis)

325th Markings

The Group flew the long tail versions of the Curtiss P-40F and P-40L Warhawk in North Africa. Settling on the 14 inch Black and Yellow checks as a group marking after experimenting with first Black and White and then Red and White checks all P-40s were marked in this fashion. The propeller spinner was painted Red. This was a theater marking and it was always used on every airplane. Numbers were in White as were serials, when they were shown before the tail markings were applied. A slight deviation from standard practice in the theater was that the numbers from 1 to 9 were not used for the headquarters flight. The 317th was assigned from 10 through 39, the 318th was allotted 40 through 69 and the 319th used 70 through 99 for its P-40s. The letter A was used after the number if two aircraft were assigned the same number. For example: 91A.

Color schemes had a bit of variety and due to a shortage of paint aircraft were flown in the scheme it carried on arrival. The standard desert scheme was Dark Earth and Midstone uppersurfaces over Azure Blue undersurfaces. Some aircraft arrived in the standard USAAF camouflage of Olive Drab uppersurfaces over Neutral Gray undersurfaces, while others were camouflaged in Sand and Olive Drab uppersurfaces over Neutral Gray. Colonel Basler even recalled some aircraft being painted in Olive Drab and Medium Green late in the campaign.

Even the national insignia varied. Some P-40s carried the standard White star on a Blue roundel, while others had the same insignia with a Yellow surround. Later all were repainted with the Star and Bar insignia, with a Red outline.

A few pilots had personal markings applied to the nose of their planes and this increased as paint became more readily available. A couple even had the wheel covers painted with personal insignias. Captain Joe Bloomer had a heart with an arrow and the word "Boss" on his wheel cover. The 318th Squadron had its Green Dragon insignia painted on the cowl of a number of its planes.

When the group converted to the Thunderbolt they were given P-47Ds, the first models being D-10s and D-11s. Later they were re-equipped with D-15s and D-16s. During one spell when a shortage of Jugs developed Colonel Sluder managed to obtain a few D-4s or D-6s, however, these simply couldn't keep up with the later models on a mission and they were soon sent to other groups.

The 325ths P-47s were camouflaged Olive Drab over Neutral Gray, the group never flew a Jug in combat in a Natural Metal finish. The size of the checks were reduced on the Thunderbolt from 14 to 12 inches.

Lieutenant Colonel Austin flew LIGHTHOUSE LOUIE, a desert camouflaged Curtiss P-40F Warhawk. The aircraft was camouflaged in Dark Earth and Midstone over Azure Blue undersides. The national insignia had a Yellow surround and the tail checks were fourteen inches. In addition the propeller spinner was painted Red as a theater marking. (G. H. Auston)

The P-47D Thunderbolts assigned to the 325th were received in the standard Olive Drab over Neutral Gray color scheme. The Red nose band was a theater marking and was applied to all group aircraft. The aircraft number was in White and the tail checks were now twelve inches. (William Carswell)

Numbering remained the same and there was at least one T-Bolt with the letter A as Colonel Sluder selected a new one to lead the group and when his old one came back from the maintenance squadron the letter A was added to the 52 on the fuselage side.

A paint shortage continued to prevent the group from applying their checker board marking scheme which had been worked out in advance

for use on the Jug. Some P-47s were flown in combat without even an aircraft identification number, but as paint was received these were quickly applied. At first only enough Yellow and Black paint was available to cover the vertical fin and tops of the horizontal stabilizers. As more lacquer was received the under surfaces were checked. The same

The early P-51B and P-51Cs were all received in overall Natural Metal with Olive Drab anti-glare panels. The theater marking consisted of a Red spinner and nose band. At first only the rudder was checked due to a shortage of paint. Later the entire fin was painted. The checks were once again reduced in size from twelve inches to ten inches. (Larry Davis)

applied to the Red nose ring. Paint was rationed to make sure that each aircraft bore the theater marking, later on the simple band was modified and swept back giving it a more racy and pleasing appearance. On the P-47s the last three digits of the serial number was carried on the fuselage side just forward of the horizontal stabilizer It was also changed from White to Yellow. The aircraft number was added to the underside of the cowling lip in White. In some cases the cowl flaps were checkered, this was used quite extensively by the 319th Squadron, but at least one Jug of the 317th bore this marking as well. The frame work of the canopy was painted Yellow on same planes, mostly those of the 318th Squadron, but a few others used this marking as well. National insignia was the standard star and bar type, with no Red surround. As with the P-40, a wide variety of names and personal markings were added to the P-47s,

While the group never flew anything but camouflaged Thunderbolts, when they switched to the P-51 Mustang they never flew one in any finish but Natural Metal. They originally were given P-51Bs and gradually P-51Ds were phased in so that at times mixed flights of both variants were sent out on missions. The tail checks were once again cut down in size from 12 inches to 10 inches. The spinners were painted Red and a Red band was painted around the nose. Numbers now were applied in Black, although some pilots had their aircraft numbers outlined in Red or Yellow for decorative purposes or to make them more readily readable in the air.

Yellow bands were added just inboard of the wing tip and just outboard of the wing fillet at about station 75 as an identification marking. Very late in the war some wing tips were checkered, and a few pilots even had the front top portion of drop tanks checked, others had the wheel well doors checkered. Still later wing tips were painted in squadron colors, Yellow for the 317th, Blue for the 318th and Red for the 319th.

Personal markings and names were used on the P-51s but art work was not as plentiful as it had been before on the P-40 and P-47. Call signs for the squadrons were Mayfair for the 317th, Inkwell for the 318th and Oatmeal for the 319th.

The Group flew P-51s using the numbers 00 and 100 which was a deviation from 15th Air Force practice. They used a few single digit numbers on aircraft. Number 5 was assigned to a P-40 and number 7 was used on several aircraft. In the case of P-51s with duplicate numbers the A was added in front of the number and was only half the size of the number.

Victory markings were pretty standard in that either Swastikas or crosses were used on all three types of aircraft. There was some individual variations as to back ground or embellishments and Italian Fascces appeared on many to denote kills over Italian aircraft.

The Partisan was a P-51D flown by the group late in the war. No record has survived as to who the pilot was or what squadron he was assigned to. The Mustang was overall Natural Metal with an Olive Drab anti-glare panel. She carried the late style of checks that went up to the leading edge of the fin extension. The nose and spinner were Red and the wingtips had Yellow bands. The engine vent panel on the lower nose was Yellow with a Black outline and the crew data plate was Black with the names of the pilot and ground crew in Yellow. The aircraft number was Black with a Yellow outline. (Checkertail Clan)